This book is dedicated to

My wife, Angela

And our children:

Joseph

Elise

Ian

Sean

William

And Silas

Without any of you, my own

story would be……. lame.

Acknowledgements

In addition to my family mentioned on the previous page, I want to thank a few friends.

Over the last few years I've had many friends, family, and strangers who have encouraged me by simply *reading* my writing. If it were possible to thank them all personally, I'd prefer that. Without that possibility in view, I thank all of them here and now. Thank you.

There are a few friends who deserve to be named here more than even those. Jay Smith, for example. Lifelong best friend, encourager of this fellow writer. The massive Red Book you gave me over ten years ago for the purpose of poking out my writing ideas is in the drawer to my left as I write. Jay, I love you, and thank you.

Matt Post, Kim Wolf, Jeana Little, and a short list of younger friends whose names will not be put here in order to protect their younger identities. All of these have been especially encouraging as I write. They have commented on my writing, asked me questions, dug into my thinking, etc. All of you— thank you.

Finally, Wanda Bolhous, of Canada. Wanda has been a friend and an editor. Her editing suggestions have helped make this entire work far more readable than it was prior to her efforts. Wanda, thank you.

What you'll find in here

Introduction

When I was a boy my mother showed me a little green booklet of poems which my great-grandmother had written. As I recall, there was nothing extraordinary about any of the writing, but *it was writing* and *it was published writing*. I was thrilled to have an ancestor who had published something—and to have known her, though for so short a time.

In a way, that little green booklet has always served as a bit of an inspiration to me. My great-grandmother wrote a book of poems. Surely I could write a book. And, for as long as I can remember, I have wanted to *write a book*.

Doesn't everyone?

This book, then, is simply the fulfillment of a dream. I have vain hopes that it will be merely the *first* fulfillment of that dream, and that I will have the gumption to write some of the many other ideas which have found their way into my cluttered cranium and onto my pen in idea form. Most of those ideas are of a very different stripe than this.

Before or after some pieces I offer a brief introduction or postlude. It is my hope that these are helpful in framing the work, giving you a fuller picture of what is happening, or that they simply add a bit more to my entertaining or thought-provoking aspirations.

~ ~ ~

To be honest, I don't have great expectations for this work. I am thrilled that you are reading it! But, having finally done what I have longed to do for so many years, I am also thrilled simply to get this far. Now, having set aside this book, I intend to pursue some of the other ideas I have been tinkering with on paper and in my mind for many months.

If three copies of this book sell, and one of those is to my mother (hmm... I really ought to just give her a freebie), I will not be shocked. In fact, there is one story within these pages that she once read and asked, "Why aren't you writing books?" That was the highest praise I could have hoped for from my mother, or any other reader.

So, while I do not have great expectations for this book, I do hope that you will laugh, cry, enjoy, and reflect as you read the words I've hammered out.

Thank you for picking this book up and giving me an opportunity to say something to you.

Mark Cheatwood

As I sat down with a pile of papers which were the many writings I intended to include in this book, I divided them into four different piles—poetry, funny stories, other types of stories, and simply thinking. This first piece comes from the 'simply thinking' pile. As I recall, I wrote this one around the same time that I attended the musical event you may read of later (if you persist in reading)—"A Taste of Glory". You may see some similarities.

The type of thinking of *The Profane* lies at the root of much of what I write.

The Profane

Profane: adj. marked by contempt or irreverence for the sacred.

I looked at a few definitions before finding this one. When I think of 'profane', I do not think of profanity, but more of the 'irreverence for' what is Good.

Have you ever come to the end of a movie and felt like Silence was the only appropriate and rightful response? That the movie was so profound, so well done, so ... *sacred*, if you will, that the best response you could possibly give would be to simply sit there, quietly, as the credits roll and the music plays?

Have you ever read a book that was so Good that the best thing you could do at the end was to gently close the book, hold it against your chest, lean back in your chair, close your eyes, and just... be... still?

Have you ever witnessed a concert, a play, or a single scene, and had a sense that applause just wasn't good enough to convey the depth of your feeling for what you just experienced? That, in fact, applause would defile the wonder of the moment?

Ever found incomprehensible Joy in a child's laugh, absolute satisfaction in a homemade cookie, unaccountable pleasure in a good conversation with a friend?

These are not *profane* moments.

These are moments of reverence, of dignity, of *the sacred*. These are moments you desire to hold onto, physically if you could, but they are of a spiritual nature. These are moments in which you stand on the precipice of something Wonderful and wish, oh how you wish, that you could physically jump into whatever sense this is. You want to feel it, to taste it, to hear it. You want it to completely overwhelm who and what you are.

These are moments of *reflection*—when you ask yourself good questions about what you just witnessed, trying to delve deeper in. They are moments you *know* were not randomly provided in your life, but that had a *higher purpose*, that they will leave behind a holy residue.

These are moments when the profane is not welcome, but sometimes comes anyway. Like an awkward joke after a beautifully worshipful moment, the profane walks up on stage and shoves holiness aside. Perhaps the real measure of just how golden that moment was is how well it sticks after the profane has tried to come in and tarnish the moment.

Perhaps.

Or... perhaps the real measure is not of 'the moment', but of *you*.

Perhaps *your* ability to discern just such a moment is the greater wonder—a grace. Perhaps there is an 'acquired taste' for such moments that some may never know, may never develop. Perhaps some folks cling to 'the Profane' to their detriment, never tasting something greater not because it is not around them, but because they cannot see it, do not hear it, do not taste it.

Having ears to hear, they do not hear. Having eyes to see, they do not see.

We can get so accustomed to junk food that real and good food does not taste good to us. We can do the same with *moments*, with life itself. We can get so accustomed to filling our heads with electronic junk data that we become almost incapable of gathering good, wholesome, *real* knowledge from everyday moments and people.

Do not get accustomed to junk food for the soul. Do not get to where you cannot recognize 'the good stuff'. Do not fill your ears and head and eyes with junk, with *the Profane*. Fill it with the good and the wonderful. Give your soul the opportunity to more fully develop, to flourish.

> *Whatever is true, or honorable, or just, or pure, or lovely, or commendable, or excellent, if there is anything worthy of praise, think about these things.*

- Philippians 4:8

~ ~ ~

It is my sincere hope that you will not find this little book 'profane', but that it will enrich your soul.

Marked for Eternity,

M

The Old Lady

Bam!

Both my wife and I sat up in bed instantly, looking around for the source of the noise. First thing I noticed was that it was 5:45 AM. The second thing was that our old dog, Daisy, was standing beside the bed looking at me expectantly. Putting two and two together, I saw that she had come through the door fast enough that it flew into the dresser behind it. That was the cause of our early morning alertness.

Scratching her head, I said some quiet words to her (they were nice words), then lay back down. She jumped into the chair in the corner of the room, circled a bit, and lay down.

Angel lay back down to sleep, too. After a few minutes I got up, grabbed my cell phone, and went downstairs. In a moment, Daisy followed me.

She and I have this thing going—when I go downstairs in the middle of the night (or, as in this case, early in the morning), she frequently tags along. If I lie down on a couch for a while, she will inevitably lie at my feet (as in *on* my feet). Seeing her stand waiting near the end of the couch, I prepared myself to be quick. The trick was to lie down and cover with a blanket in the same instant, or else, as happened early on in these little encounters, she would be lying down on my feet before the blanket got in place.

Having successfully accomplished my mission, she was on my blanket-covered feet before my head was on the pillow.

~ ~ ~

We were just talking the other day about how long she's been with us. We concluded she had been born in May of 2001, twelve years ago. Angel looked up the breed—English Springer Spaniel—and found two sources that indicated they lived twelve to fourteen years.

[sigh]... she's an old lady.

~ ~ ~

Wasn't long ago that I didn't think we should look for another dog. One son kept saying we ought to, because Daisy wouldn't be around much longer. Get her to train the new pup, he said.

And, perhaps she would. Someone has to tell the new guy where the road is, where to find coons and skunks when they are hunting our chickens, and how to chase chickens off the back porch (but only when the master is looking).

Then, after a while, I had the same notion, and admitted to it. It bothered me, but... it did seem like something we ought to do. Angel was still reluctant. The other day, though... she was looking at puppies.

~ ~ ~

Always happens.

After a few minutes of lying on my feet, Daisy decides that such a position isn't as comfortable as she had hoped. She climbs off the couch, but doesn't go far. Plopping down near the end of the couch, she goes right back to sleep.

Poor old lady.

~ ~ ~

Not sure I'm ready for another dog. I really doubt Daisy can handle it. We took her to be bred once... that did *not go well*. Fortunately, she didn't rip the flesh off of that other dog. She does okay with kittens and cats. Even MamaCat (yes, that's her name) has gotten accustomed to her... uh... sniffing.

~ ~ ~

I got off the couch, got my shower, and was leaving the bathroom when I found her lying right outside the bathroom door, waiting. I stepped over her. She kept sleeping.

Sometimes I find myself watching her closely, just to make sure she still breathes. Those times come far more often of late.

And, yes, as I walked over her sleeping form in the darkness, this particular sleep was not permanent. While I could chest rise and fall in her breathing, the sound of her snoring told the story.

~ ~ ~

The other day one of the kids said they thought Daisy was deaf. At least partially. So, because none of us were quite sure, we tested the theory.

We called her. Nothing.

We clapped our hands. Nothing.

She did still respond to whistles.

Fading....

~ ~ ~

It was one of the boys who noticed the large family of raccoons in the yard. He charged into the room, shouted "Coons!" and most of us ran outside. One son got the shotgun, another a .22.

I grabbed a hoe. Trust me on this—this old man has taken care of chicken-killing fiends with a hoe before.

Before the night was done, there were many coons who would *not* be eating chickens on this glorious evening. And Daisy, old Daisy, had been inside the whole time. We came into the house to find her sleeping on a chair. Perhaps she was too tired for such hunting and glory. Perhaps she didn't smell them, didn't hear us rushing out of the house. Perhaps she didn't even startle when my son had rushed in yelling, "Coons!"

There was something funny about that level of inattention, but... something sad, too. It was yet another reminder that our time with her was not long.

~ ~ ~

I remember when she was young. We lived in a small town called Laura, in town, and she was confined to our house and a small, fenced in yard. She was always getting out and needing to be chased. She longed to run free, and, as a younger dog, she was *not* easy to catch. The town park was right next to our house—it had plenty of room to run. When we weren't irritated with having to try to catch her, we could just stand there and watch her. The energy, the freedom... it was kind of cool to see, really. But we just wanted her back in the yard.

"Daisy! Come!"

She didn't listen *then*, either, come to think of it. But back then it wasn't because she was deaf.

When we moved to the house a few miles outside of Troy, her life changed. We never had to fence her in again. She roamed at will, but seemed to understand the basic boundaries instinctively. With room to run, she was happier than we ever knew she could be. That freedom we saw back in the park was an everyday thing for her.

She has been on the road in front of our house a few times. It is pretty busy for a country road. But the only time she ever gets on that road is when we are walking out there ourselves. Even then she is usually hesitant, but some things have provoked her. If you are a biker, and we are walking out to get the mail, just know—you are the enemy.

Other than that, she runs freely. We were all really happy for her when we saw her running, playing in puddles, chasing rabbits, digging out moles. She was at home here. It was a good thing. Daisy had found her home.

Now, she is still at home, but she doesn't seem to enjoy it as much as she used to. I haven't seen her in a dead run after a rabbit in a while. She does still do an occasional whimper at a mole hole, and some digging.

~ ~ ~

Two of our boys don't remember life without her. William was not a year-and-a-half when she came. Silas... wasn't. Because of that, I do wonder whether her eventual death will be particularly hard on them. To all of us she is family. But, for them, she is family without whom they have no memories.

~ ~ ~

There's another coon out there somewhere. But she will not find it. I will, or one or more of the boys. We need to find it before it relieves us of more chickens. Infernal thing. We will dispatch it when we catch it. They still hide in the upper beams of the barn, believing that they are safe from the dog there. Well, they are, but ... they may find themselves safe from her on the floor, too.

Too tired, too old, she just doesn't chase down bothersome critters anymore. No, wait... come to think of it, Elise did have to bathe her after an interaction with a skunk last spring.

But, inevitably, the day will come. We will be sitting together watching a movie, eating popcorn, laughing, enjoying. The movie will end, we'll rush through the credits just in case something quirky is at the end, we'll have a collective "aw" in disappointment and turn off the television. We'll chatter for a few minutes, then get up, turn the lights off, wait for her, and discover... that she breathes no more.

There will be sadness. I cannot deny it. There is sadness in my heart right now just seeing that in our future. Great sadness, but we are being prepared for it as we watch her diminish.

Today, though, she will run in the grass, lie on the bank of the barn waiting for us to return home, and come trotting to the van when we arrive. She will climb stairs and couches with decreasing agility and speed.

Today, we will love on her, and she will love us right back. She always does.

Today, she will breathe.

Love Never Fails

Lying in bed after a full, but good day
I was slowly drifting off to sleep.
She finished reading
Turned off her light
And slid down into the covers

A moment later
She wordlessly reached her hand out
Took my hand
And held it

Thus, she fell asleep

I, however, did not.
Her action had stirred me
It meant something
Many somethings
And I was going to take those things in
deeply.

It meant *love*.

She knows how much it means to me to have even the simplest
Touch from her. Call it a 'love language', if you will. I was
hearing her say, in the quietest, most profound way, "I love
you." These were words which were often spoken, but... this
action spoke them in a language akin to angelic song.

It meant *grace, mercy, forgiveness.*

Twenty-three years of marriage did not come without its pains, offenses, and blatant wrongs. Birthdays and anniversaries uncelebrated, angry and foolish words, so many of the uglier moments of life. The things I had done to her, the hurt I had put her through, the pains I had caused her—*forgiven*. They had been forgiven all along the path, yes, but this hand in this moment was reminding me of the mercies of the past. Our past.

It meant *hope*.

This hand symbolized, to me, the fact that she had not lost hope. She had lost hope, I had lost hope, but we were both stubborn enough to find it again. We are both drawing nearer to the Lord, we both experience changes in positive ways, we both mature. Life ahead is looking well, though we see physical and financial challenges coming. Our hope grows. Together.

It meant *respect*.

I sensed this mainly because she was 'speaking' my language. This, *touch*, was not her language, but my own. By reaching her hand out to hold mine, she was walking into my Rome and doing as I do.

I could go on. The moment was infused with meaning in my mind and heart. It reminded me of all that was good and right in the world. It gave me a quiet, settled, resolved peace. It made a tired man lie there without sleep, not because his mind was filled with anxieties, but because it was filled with wonder and joy and love.

I was... *happy*.

Every moment is so filled with thoughts and actions and memories—of things that have been said and done and thought before. But some of the best of Good moments are also filled with Intention. When Angel reached her hand out to hold mine, she Intended to do so. Such an action reminds me that...

Love never fails.

As you read you may notice that these stories are not in chronological order. For example, in that last section my wife and I had been married for 23 years. We are now, as I write, past our 28th anniversary. This next story is from many years past. In the early 90s we lived in Arkansas. For two years I worked for a shipping company whose employees primarily wore brown. Occasionally I would come home with stories of the personalities there. This story is one of my personal favorites. It is entirely true (except, maybe, the last sentence). The fact that it is entirely true is stunning. Who was it who said 'truth is stranger than fiction"? Well, this story is evidence that the quote is true.

By the way, I have changed the names of these characters—not because I am trying to protect the 'innocent' (such beings do not exist), but because I don't want a lawsuit.

Did I say that out loud?

Nobody Loved Brandon

One job I held when I was living in the furnace commonly referred to as "Arkansas" was at a large shipping company. I won't say who they were, but I never thought brown was an attractive color, so I didn't stay too long.

One of my peers often referred to himself as "six feet one inches, two hundred pounds, of beautiful, manly muscle." His ego was fragile enough that most folks simply left it alone. The reality of the situation was this—he was closer to five foot nine, two hundred forty pounds, and it included a goodly portion of flabby tissue.

This was not his only delusion, though. Besides the taller, trimmer, more muscular apparition he saw in the mirror, there was also a brain that could out-think Einstein. He thought he was *brilliant*.

Okay, so he didn't *say* Einstein. He did say that he could be the president of the United States, that he could run the Fortune 500 company we worked at together better than the folks who were running it, that he could write a best-selling novel if he wanted to, that... well, perhaps you get the picture. No matter what it was, he could do it better, faster, brighter, higher. And he said it in so many ways, so often, and so tirelessly.

Well, tirelessly for *him*. The rest of us were *rather* tired of it.

I find, though, that you can put up with lots of nonsense when a person works hard, diligently does his part, shows up for work on time, comes to work every day, persists when times are hard, endures to the end, keeps going when everyone else is gasping for breath, pulls more than his weight, performs seeming miracles, does the unexpected, and shows himself to be an unbelievably great team player.

Brandon, of course, did none of these things.

Wait. That's neither accurate nor fair. He *did* do the unexpected.

In fact, one of my favorite Brandon stories was of the hot summer night (in Arkansas that would be a redundancy) that my boss did *not* give Brandon the night off when he begged for it with more energy than that with which he usually worked. He didn't request it ahead of time, per the rules. He just walked in and demanded it. Well, when the boss didn't give in, he fussed and fumed and stomped around like an out-of-control toddler.

Our shift was all of four hours long. We usually worked about two hours, took a fifteen minute break, and then worked about two more. We worked until all of the boxes at our work station were sorted into racks that moved around the line. Each boxline had about a third of the addresses of the surrounding area—the area supported by our station. We had to know what color of cage into which to put each address and which level (high, middle, low).

Ours was not as physically demanding of a job as the folks who unloaded truck trailers. They had to keep three different boxlines working, so they had to move three times as many boxes as we did. However, we had to memorize a lot of addresses. Ours was skilled labor! No, literally, it was considered skilled labor, so we got paid a buck more per hour.

Each boxline usually had three workers at a time. The slide was on our right, the moving boxline on our left. All night we would move boxes from our right to our left. Right, left, right, left, right, left, right, left. If we were inordinately bored, we might turn around and do a Left to Right for a while, but that always felt awkward.

Nick was usually at the front of our boxline. He liked it up there, and had been around for a long time, so he kind of got his choice. That and he intimidated Brandon by being snarly and intelligent. This was Nick's second job. He had been working here as a box sorter for 11 years. His day job was something he did in an office for the state, downtown. He was just biding his time in both jobs as he waited for his chance to be a driver—a wearer of brown.

He was Greek, grumpy-looking, and I liked him. I didn't agree with him on much, but we really enjoyed bantering. Oh, the Nick stories... I may have to do that one day. For example, I'd have to tell about how I had told my wife how grumpy he was, how he rarely ever smiled, and that every Nick story included some comment about his scowling appearance. Then, the day she first met him at a church festival he had invited me to. His brilliant smile that day was perplexing to me—was this a twin? Who was this man?

But today's Nick wasn't that one. On our boxline I was usually in the middle or at the back. I had less seniority, so I ended up wherever the others didn't want to be. On this infamous night, Brandon had chosen to be in the back. He often chose the back, because he could be a slacker without our easily detecting his crummy behavior.

However, tonight he wanted to be noticed.

I was working away early in the shift—right to left, right to left—when I heard a bit of an unusual bang. Our work was a noisy place. We had big metal boxes going around about a 150 foot long, oval-shaped line, conveyor belts moving all over the building, trucks pulling in and out, fork-lifts, horns, etc. There was a lot of noise. A bang doesn't necessarily mean anything. So, when I first heard the bang it didn't seem too out of the ordinary.

When I heard it a second time, it was louder, more obvious.

I turned around and saw Brandon lying on the steel grate floor. He was just lying there. This might not be good, I thought, and called out to Nick.

"Hey!"

He turned around, I pointed at Brandon, and we both moved slowly towards his immobile person. Nick ('Nicholas' to Brandon—"My friends call me Nick. Brandon, *you* can call me *Nicholas*.") and I stood above Brandon's "unconscious" body. We looked down at him for a moment, then at each other. I bent down and tried to wake him. I shook him a little, called his name, but no response. I stood back up; Nick and I walked aside a bit, and quietly conferred.

"He's faking it," Nick said.

"Yup".

Nick told me to go get the boss. Then, he turned and continued working the boxline.

We left Brandon lying on the steel grate floor.

When I returned with the boss, I couldn't help noticing that Brandon, who had been "unconscious" the whole time, was no longer lying with his head on the steel great flooring, but was conveniently lying on his arm.

What a fascinating study, this man.

The boss came, Nick and I worked extra hard to make up for our "unconscious" peer (wasn't much difference in terms of work accomplished, really), and the boss, who had some medical training, tried to wake Brandon. To no avail.

Are you surprised? Well, we weren't.

The boss called Nick and I downstairs for a few minutes—out of earshot of "the body."

"I am going to have to call the ambulance," the boss said.

Nick erupted. "He's a --- ------ ------- faker!"

And so on.

The boss said he knew that, but he didn't have any choice in the matter. Rules were rules. We talked a bit, fumed over our *once again* having to make up for Brandon's lazy incompetence, and got back to work.

The paramedics arrived about 10 minutes later. Somehow, Brandon continued to be unconscious. On his arm. The ambulance drove right into our building. Nick and I had a lot of work to catch up on, so we didn't bother watching—for the most part. The boss was good enough to get us a helper for a while, so we could catch up. We did turn around once in a while to see the paramedics hovering around Brandon's limpid frame. (Did I mention there wasn't much difference? Yes? Oh, okay.)

Later, the boss filled us in on what was happening behind us.

The paramedics, who also could tell it was a hoax, gave Brandon a sternum rub. Apparently they did this in order to wake folks who had inexplicably passed out. The unconscious Brandon, ever the brilliant actor, couldn't stand the sternum rub, so, *with both hands* (one of which had been lying under his head, remember) smacked away the sternum-rubbing knuckles. And, in a tremendously fascinating case study in the need for unconscious people to be comfortable, after brushing off those sternum-rubbing knuckles, he put one of his hands back under his head so he wouldn't have to lie on that uncomfortable grate.

The boss said that the first time Brandon pulled this off, he almost forgot to put his hand back there. He let his hands just fall limply back to the ground, noticeably felt his head resting on the grates, then quickly lifted his head back up and moved one unconscious hand back behind his head.

The paramedics were dumbfounded.

This ridiculous scene happened *five times*—until the paramedics couldn't take it anymore. They left Brandon lying (in so many ways) and went downstairs to laugh their heads off. Oh, and to figure out their next move.

They ended up taking him away in the ambulance. Again, rules were rules.

We were disgusted with the whole thing.

Nick and I got some help for the rest of the night. Brandon's acting debut had taken about an hour. He won no awards, didn't even get a nomination. But, he did manage to get the last three hours of the night off.

Good thing, too. He probably still made it to that Boy George concert on time.

I wrote this just prior to having our two oldest leave home for two different college experiences. The oldest had been through two years of college locally, but was pursuing a dream of attending a fairly new college in which our family had a vested interest. Both ended up leaving home within a week of each other.

This piece was me writing out some of the things buzzing around in my head and heart as I prepared for the moment when our family would no longer be the same—an adventurous and fun time, but something quite different than what we had before.

It was only yesterday...

It was only yesterday that...

He ran ahead on a trail in the woods, brimming with excitement
We watched him, noticing the change in a young boy *outdoors*
He wandered off the trail constantly
Following tracks, looking at plants, chasing frogs
I showed him how to skip rocks, and could do it with him for ages

It was only yesterday that...

She had curly red hair that bounced when she ran
Which she did often
We watched her do everything quicker than the first child

She stood up on her feet and began running... into tables and
walls
We were astonished at the difference between the two

It was only yesterday that...

He watched me show my anger and frustration by hitting a wall
with my fist
Then, to my horror, he curled up his chubby one-year old fist
and did likewise
He was much slower to start walking, but when he finally
started he never made a mistake
We still laugh about the differences...

It was only yesterday that...

They both ran alongside the creek, stopping to watch critters
and bugs
I learned from them even then, because *they were not afraid*
They watched as I butchered chickens for the very first time...
They watched from behind a window
Because I didn't know what would happen next

It was only yesterday that...

They worked with me, side by side, as we cut and hauled wood
to heat our home
They worked hard, laughed lots, and came home with stories
for Mom
He has always come *alive* in the woods in ways that still amaze
me
She has a heart of gold that calls for kindly mining operations

It was only yesterday that...

He was tinkering with a hammer and tongs, starting his first fire on a forge
He was working hard for *hours* trying to make a skin into good leather
She touched a piano for the very first time, and something happened inside
She stepped outside to volunteer and meet people elsewhere

It was all only yesterday. Wasn't it only yesterday?

And, now, so many years have fallen away, nothing left but memories that fail
My heart breaks as I look to tomorrow, which is only a few days away
There will be holes in my home which nobody else can fill
Sounds, Words, Stories, Memories... holes in my heart that yearn...

It was only yesterday. Tomorrow is coming soon.

As much as it pains me, as much as it hurts their mother,
New Lives are in the making—and we *are* excited to see
Just what will happen next? What Yesterdays are about to be created?
What simple, elegant, beautiful, awesome wonders are about to be New in our history?

I cherish Yesterday, but I will also cherish the Yesterdays that are yet to be...

It was only yesterday that I held him in my arms for the very first time
I had *no idea* for *years* just how wonderful that time was
It was only yesterday that I held her in my arms for the very first time
I had no idea that this would be my only daughter. Ever.

It was only yesterday...

I will cherish those memories with every breath
While we move onward in different lives
Creating new Yesterdays as we go
In lives that are new and different

After my Brown experience, I turned Purple. I've been Purple longer than some of our children have been alive. After a few years of driving for Purple, I entered operations management. This is one story from that time.

I need a manager on line one

"I need a manager on line one, please, a manager on line one."

Some things are simply a part of your responsibility, so you do them, even if you don't like it. I hated answering these phone calls—even the good ones. When the call begins with something like "I need a manager on line one…" it is so rarely a *good* call. Compliments typically go unsaid, whereas complaints do not.

It was a customer. She had been waiting for a package that had not come. When I found out where she lived, I knew it was more than an hour from the station. It was getting late in the day (shortly before 5:00), she had grocery shopping to do, and she had a football game to attend that evening. She had to have this package for something happening in the morning. Could I find out what was going on?

Absolutely!

Airbill number in hand, I found the package, carried it back to my office, and let the customer know we would find a way to get it there *tonight*. My quick research had shown that the customer was well off the edge of the normal Saturday delivery area, so I knew sending it out the next morning would *not* get it in her hands on time.

I had no drivers at my disposal. All of the night drivers were already on routes for the evening. It was a Friday evening, too, so all the day folks had been clearing out as quickly as they arrived. So, when I looked around the station, I saw only one guy who was an option.

Me.

Pre-trip the van. Leave word with the customer service agents. Gone.

In order to keep tabs on what was happening on the road while I was away from the office for two hours, I turned on the van's radio. Not much chatter was going on in the courier ranks that evening, which was good news.

An hour later, the package was delivered, and we had a satisfied customer who was thrilled to see us go out of our way to help. On my way back to the station the radio got busy. We had a courier who was having some technical difficulties. The conversation with dispatch sounded like it had been going on for a bit. Perhaps I had missed something while chatting with the customer for a few minutes.

Courier: "I haven't received any transmissions for more than an hour."

Dispatch: "You have three stops that are closing shortly."

The courier appeared to know about two of the three, and was en route to one. It was now six o'clock. All three stops were closing at six. I realized that the courier was the one from the area I was going to be driving through shortly, so I got on the radio and offered to take a stop.

When I arrived at the location, a strip mall, it was 6:15. The stop had been closed for fifteen minutes. It was on the end of this strip mall, had a front that was entirely window and nobody appeared to be present. I hustled to the door, tried it, found it locked, and tried to look around desks and the counter—hoping to see *someone*.

Nobody.

But, I did see the package. It was a letter, lying on the counter, about six feet from the door.

Alright, I thought, now I just need to find a way to get my hands on it. I shook the door. It didn't give. I looked around for an alarm or a camera. My thought was that, if I set off an alarm, I would get that package. No alarm was apparent.

Quickly, I went to a neighboring store and asked questions. They did not have a key, did not have phone numbers for any of the people who worked there, did not know anybody. They didn't know whether a janitorial service would show up.

Walking around the building, I checked for other doors to the facility. I found other doors, but they were just as hopelessly locked as the front door.

I, on the other hand, was *not* hopeless. I could see that package, and I was going to find a way to get it to where it needed to be.

Standing on the sidewalk in front of the storefront, I contemplated other options. I looked through the window, trying to find any kind of phone number that may be posted and helpful, looked for a bulletin board nearby ... anything that would give me helpful information.

Then, I saw it—a mail slot in the door.

Heh heh heh. Bingo.

My arm didn't fit through very well, but I could get it partially through. I opened the back of the van to start looking for potential resources. What if I tore up a couple empty letters, found a way to bind them together? What if I did that with boxes? Did I have any spare wires somewhere? Was there a part of the supply rack that I could dismantle and use? Did I have a hanger? Or three?

At this point, a man walked by who had been at a neighboring store. He could tell I was not a thief (maybe the company truck was a bit of a clue), and was intrigued by what was going on.

"Anything I can do for you?"

"Not unless you have a wire about eight feet long. Got that?"

"No, sorry. What are you trying to do?"

I pointed out the package sitting on the counter. "I want that."

"Dude."

He watched as a light bulb turned on in my head, and I began tearing up a document crate—because it had a stiff wire around the rim! In a few minutes I had straightened the wire. It appeared to reach about five-and-a-half feet. If I could get my arm in that slot a bit further... it just might work.

The man watched as I pushed the wire through the mail slot, shoved my arm in past the elbow, and began reaching for that package. Stretch….

"What if an alarm goes off?" he asked.

"I'm good with that. My guess is that I'd get the package at that point."

He laughed out loud. "This is amazing and cool," he said. "It'd make a *great* commercial."

I laughed at that, and replied, "Unfortunately, it would have to start with, 'The courier was *late*.'"

He laughed again. "Yeah, I guess that takes away some of the punch."

I reached the package with the end of the wire, pulled at it… and it fell to the floor.

"Augh!" I said.

He moaned a bit. "Now what?"

I had come this far, there was *no way* it was over. Not yet.

Again, I was rummaging in the back of the van. Multi-piece labels were sticky. That was the ticket. Sticky, small. I took a couple off the sheet, rolled them, and attached them securely to the end of my wire.

"Wow," the main said.

Again, I reached the wire through the mail slot, shoved my arm in, and proceeded toward the letter. Reaching it, I tried to press the sticky label onto the letter—enough that it would hold. Slowly, I began to lift the letter into the air, and pull the wire back…

"Steady…" the man offered, mesmerized as he watched.

Slowly, I drew the wire back through the mail slot, careful not to shake it. When it was almost to the door… I reached carefully through the mail slot with my other hand and snagged it.

Success!

The man was cheering. Apparently, this whole scene had made his day. It had certainly made mine.

The letter went out that night, as it had been planned. I don't know whether that customer ever knew how close we came to messing that up for them. I never heard a thing about it from anybody. As far as I know someone may have walked into the office that next morning, saw the blank space on the counter where the letter had been, and thought nothing of it.

That wire is in my office to this day—a quiet reminder, sitting in the corner, of what my persistence needs to look like.

While we lived in Arkansas there were times when I needed to find extra work to meet our young family's needs. One of my favorite side jobs was yard work. Not only have I always loved cutting grass, but customers provide good stories. Mr. Frost, whose real name is actually close to his fictional name in this story, and fits his character (as displayed here), was my first customer one summer.

Yard Customer #1 – Mr. Frost

One summer, I decided to start my own lawn business. In addition, I was working a part time job handling packages and taking classes at college. So, I put an advertisement in the paper. The phone did not ring off the hook, but... it did, eventually, ring.

The man on the other end of the line said his name was Emerson Frost.

"I am calling in regard to your newspaper advertisement."

His speech was eminently enunciated.

We discussed things a bit, I wrote out directions to his house, noted the address, made an appointment to meet, and ended our phone call.

This was the first response to my ad, but I had hopes of getting 10 or 20 customers for the summer. Mr. Frost's yard was all the way across town, which would be a good place to start. It was a good neighborhood, plenty of potential. I would go out there, give a reasonable bid, do a good job, and hope that he had friends who also needed work done.

A few days later I was walking around Mr. Frost's yard trying to figure out how much time it would take to cut his grass. It wasn't an especially big yard, but it wasn't small. I decided it would take me about an hour. Having already decided I would aim for about twenty dollars per hour, my bid was easy.

I walked up to the door, knocked, and waited.

Mr. Frost was probably in his early 60s, of medium height, medium build. His hair was white, not gray. Either he was a widower or his wife was an invalid confined to the house—I do not recall. I do remember seeing some family pictures when he let me in the kitchen once that summer, but more about that moment… in a moment.

We stood and talked pleasantries for a couple minutes. It was only May or June at the time, so the blistering heat of Arkansas hadn't hit yet. Pleasantries were still pleasant out of doors.

Then I told him I would cut his yard for twenty dollars per cut.

The look on his face concerned me. He looked seriously perplexed, perhaps dumb-founded. Had I over-priced? Surely not. Surely he did not think so. If twenty dollars was too much for this yard, then I was going to have a hard time making any money on this idea. A very hard time. Twenty dollars?

"I'm sorry, Mark, but I cannot pay you twenty," he said.

Oh, boy, I thought. I wondered what else I might do to provide for our young family, but I wasn't about to go lower.

"It's just not enough. How about thirty-five?"

This time the perplexity was on my own face. If I had the ability to raise a single eyebrow in a questioning sort of way, I would have done so at that moment. However, not having said ability, I did not. Instead, I just stood there with my mouth gaping open, my mind frozen, looking like an idiot.

"Mark?"

Snap out of it, goober, I said to myself.

"Sir," I finally stuttered, "I can't do that to you."

"Then I am afraid I cannot hire you."

This was certainly not something I had envisioned—losing a bid because my bid wasn't high enough? What?

"How about twenty-five?" I asked.

We ended up at thirty. What can I say? The man drove a hard bargain.

So, over the next several weeks I would come out to Mr. Frost's house, cut the grass, trim the edges, talk for a few minutes, collect, and head onward. In our little conversations along the way I learned that he was a Christian, specifically a Methodist. I learned a little about his career, his family, etc.

One day when I drove up the driveway he was out working in the flower beds. I noticed that he wasn't moving around quite as easily as usual, so I asked him about it before getting to work on the yard.

"Mark, I'm afraid I've done something to my back."

We talked about it a bit. He had a chiropractor, had an appointment set up for a few days away, etc. He indicated that he was concerned that something was bad enough that he may need surgery. I expressed regret and told him that I would pray for him. He headed for the house; I went to do the yard work.

As I was cutting the grass, I kept feeling compelled to offer to pray *with* him prior to leaving. This wasn't normal for me with folks I did not know, but... it seemed like the right thing to do. When I finished in the yard, I went to the door and knocked. Mr. Frost opened the door.

"Sir, I'm done out here. I was wondering whether it would be okay if I prayed with you about your back."

At this point, I was once again seeing the incredulous look. In fact, it may have been something more like... all out fear.

"Uh...", he said, "o...kay." This was probably the worst constructed sentence I ever heard the man speak in all the time I worked for him.

He looked cautiously around the neighborhood as though we were suddenly engaged in covert operations—as if we were preparing to do a drug deal. He anxiously stepped backward into the house. He motioned for me to follow him into the house, and, I had the impression, to do so quickly. Next, he swiftly closed the door behind me—so we could proceed with our... evil plan?

It wasn't until later that it dawned on me—he didn't really want me in his house, but he certainly didn't want to be seen having prayer in the yard!

After closing the door, he turned to me and said, "Okay?" I had the impression he was asking me whether this was a safe place for our dirty deed.

Now, I'd spent some time with charismatic friends, as well as read some good books. I'd prayed with friends for years. I thought this moment would call for a hands-on approach. Knowing that Mr. Frost was a Christian, and having more of a John Wesley thought of what I knew of as "Methodist" than what was then actually Methodist, I stepped towards him to pray. His eyes went wide and he quickly moved to put the kitchen table between us. I didn't take the hint the first time (I'm rather slow that way), so I moved around towards him again.

He circled the wagons. Or the table.

After a few of these movements, I finally got the idea that the 'laying on of hands' was not what Mr. Frost, no true spiritual descendent of John Wesley, had in mind. In fact, I became increasingly concerned that he was thinking I was more of a mugger than a pray-er. So, I stopped the chase, stood still, looked him in the eye, bowed my head, closed my eyes, and prayed.

After the brief prayer, he awkwardly moved towards the door. In a moment, we were back outside. He paid me for the yard work, and I was on my way to the truck.

"Mark", he called.

I stopped and turned towards him. "Yes, sir?"

"Thanks for praying for me."

"Any time, sir. Really." And I was gone.

It was a stretch for me to do what I did there—offering to pray with a virtual stranger, a man whose spiritual condition I knew not. But ... it was a good stretch.

In time, Mr. Frost would give me the address of a friend who wanted me to look at his yard and give a quote. His friend's name, and I'm not making this up, was Colonel Petty. But ... that's another story.

The night I describe in this story was one in which I was transfixed. The artists whose work brought this on may be an irrelevant point, but I did enjoy their performance. Such a passion has happened to many, I'm sure, in observances of Handel's Messiah and other greater works.

A Taste of Glory

Last night my family and I had the absolute pleasure of attending a performance of "Leahy, a Celtic Christmas". I had never heard of the Leahy family previously but... will never forget them. If you *ever* have the opportunity to see this musically gifted family, do yourself and your children a favor— spend what it takes.

There are so many things I could say about the show, but... it seems to me that none of the things I could say would portray to you anything close to the meaning and value that I found in it. I will say this—I had never thought of the simple and Christ-less song as Holy... but last night I tasted Glory even during "Jingle Bells".

So many songs brought me to tears. I was in awe for most of the evening. At one point I found myself looking into the air, toward the high ceilings of the auditorium... looking for signs of angels. Such a sense of the Glory of God was upon me that I wondered whether there were any *visible* signs of Him.

Crazy? Okay.

As the performance continued, my mind was drawn to other thoughts of the Glory of God. I briefly thought about the "shadows" mentioned in Hebrews. All of this beauty I was experiencing was *nothing* in comparison to the heavenly music we would one day enjoy. It was all nothing in comparison to the Glory in Whose Presence we will stand, kneel, and lie prostrate.

Yes, we are living in the shadow lands.

I spent time contemplating the wonders that we taste in this life that give us hints of Glory, a taste of the Glory yet to come. I think every pleasure of this life is a hint of That One, every longing is for something Other, every desire is actually for something Holy and Wonderful that is j-u-s-t—o-u-t—o-f—r-e-a-c-h.....

That weekend, as I sat eating cheesecake my wife had made for my birthday, I tasted every single bite slowly, deliberately, wonderfully, as fully as I knew how to cherish. I knew that I was tasting something akin to Glory.

Even writing this I find that I am writing in the shadows. None of my words say enough. That night during the show it got to the point that clapping didn't seem to convey enough of what I wanted to express. At the end of the performance I felt... almost like a baptism had occurred. I felt like I had been washed. Such a sense of peace... joy... refreshment.

I had a very quiet drive home... peacefully listening to the chatter in the van as we drove thirty miles home that late and cold night. I felt ... wonderful.

Heavenly things are well beyond what I can currently grasp, but I am enjoying the things that God has put in my life. I am going to enjoy them, recognize them as the unfathomable gifts that they are, and identify them as tastes of Glory *now*—recognizing that there is so much more that is yet to come.

~ ~ ~

Recently I heard a man say that he saw a beautiful sunset, but was struck by something outside of it—a thought. That thought was this—no matter how wonderful a particular sunset may be, it is broken.

There's something more beautiful and majestic waiting for us.

Wow.

Growing Older

A six year old boy
Plays on the swings
As his father works nearby

Removing old windows
For Spring had come
Time for the old house
To breath

Pulling out a window
The man hears a cry
"Hey, Dada! Look!"

Turning, he saw
What struck his heart
With pain
As well
As with pleasure

His youngest child
Swung freely
Of his own accord

Huzzahs were offered
On the outside
But inside
The man died
A little

Gone were the days
Of a child crying out
For a push
On a swing

This last child
Having learned the kick
Would leave this old man
With pushes remaining

His old arms and back
Would still have the strength
For more children
On swings

But now his own children
All grown older
No longer required
That strength

Oldest to youngest
All now swinging
Without the assistance
Of Dad

But there are other
Types of pushing
Other types
Of swings
This father
Is not done

Not yet.

Spider in the Shower!

I stepped into my morning shower
And saw a spider whose brow did glower

I stepped aside to keep away
And fretted on how I had begun my day

I washed my hair
It was still there!

I washed my face
It was still in place!

I closed my eyes
It grew in size!

I shaved my face
It rushed me with haste!

Aaaaaaaaaaaaaaaaahhhh! I screamed!
Then stomped & creamed......

....

Well. That wasn't so bad.
I hope you're not sad.

A few days back I was reminiscing with an old friend and one of his sons about our times at Boy Scout camp near Camden, Ohio. My good friend and I had gone there together as scout leaders and dads for many years, but our time had come to an end when his sons were done with scouts and my middle boys chose to do theater in their summers.

This is one story that we talked about as we got caught up that Saturday evening. An old favorite.

The Day Tarzan Visited Walmart. Well, Almost.

I could hardly be blamed, really. I mean, the Tarzan Yell had become so ingrained in me throughout a pounding, grueling, physically challenging, emotionally roller coastering week that it was second nature. So, there I stood, in front of the cereal at Walmart, taking a quick, deep breath, and...

Holy smokes.

~ ~ ~

It was Boy Scout week once again—one of my two favorite weeks of the year. Every year, for ten years, I had attended Boy Scout camp with our Pleasant Hill, Ohio troop—Troop 146. It had all started when Joseph, our oldest, was not quite a teen, and it wrapped up when Ian was barely into his Boy Scout years. The end of my Boy Scout camp years was a very sad thing for me. The troop had been dwindling in numbers for a while. All the boys who were in the troop during Joseph's time were well past the age of 18, many guys who had joined in at the same time as Ian had slunk away without completing much, and the Sean's-age kids had, apparently, very little or no interest.

Sad, really. Boy Scouts had more to offer in the 'life skills' department than any program running. Soccer had nothing more than competitive jogging to offer; theater would help you overcome the fear of public speaking, and a bit more; other sports were ... well, singularly focused on that sport. Scouts offered a wide variety of skills.

Anyway, that year at Scout camp we started something. Every year became a fantastic time in its own way. Every year included some of the ritual, habitual things that we did as a troop. But some years brought something new to *who we were*.

Take, for example, the "QUARANTINED" lid. For years the troop's Scout Master (the guys and I referred to him as 'The Wise One', amongst other honorable titles) would do tent inspections. The winners were the ones who, in his exceptionally good judgment, had the cleanest tents. Before coming to camp, he would prepare five stakes for the daily winners of this competitive award.

Monday afternoon it would start. After the boys were off to their merit badge classes of various types, he would walk through camp checking out the condition of all the tents. The winners would have the day's stake hammered into the ground at the base of their tent. In our troop that was a *big deal.* I've run into boys, now men, years afterward and learned that they still have those stakes.

Well, that was one tradition that never went away. One year, though, we added a little something to it. One day a buddy and

I were doing the inspections, and we found one campsite to be *particularly* bad. Not satisfied to have it be a mere conversation later, we decided that we would do more.

Our boys thrived on competitive banter, competitive achievement. They wanted to win. They liked winning. They were, did I mention, competitive. As a troop we had been able to use that competitive nature well—to improve our campsite for future campers, to create teamwork, to diminish selfishness. Many things, really. The cleanest tent award itself had become so competitive with our boys that it had begun to go well beyond 'cleanest tent'. During the best and brightest years, every single tent would be clean. We would be *looking* for dirt (at a campground), leaves (in the woods), and things that were out of place. A single wrapper from a small candy bar, a poorly tied doorway, a small clump of dirt, a crooked pillow—all of these things could lose your tent the day's stake.

On this day we encountered a pair of youths who hadn't cared about having a clean tent, who seemed to be rubbing this whole 'best tent award' idea in the mud.

Having decided a conversation wasn't enough, we sat and gave it some thinking. No. We would do something that would cause their peers to apply righteous peer pressure.

We dug around in the troop trailer for something to emblemize the issue. Glory be, we found an unused, old, dented trash can lid. Then, finding a black marker, we simply wrote, "QUARANTINED" on the lid, threw the lid into the middle of the site in question, and left it.

Oh man. A ruckus was raised, laughter roared, boys felt the competitive fires of their peers, and there wasn't another one of *those* messes all week. Even the victims of the award loved the idea... eventually.

Another difference-maker in our weeks one year was the "Scout Master Splash". Early in Joseph's time the event was fairly lame. It was usually old, fat Scout Masters or other adult leaders taking part in a cannon ball plunge at the end of the otherwise Olympian events. There would be members of the camp staff who would judge the event based on 'style' as well as splash. Leading up to this event the scouts would participate in a long-distance foot race, bike race, bow and arrow shooting, boat racing, etc. Each event would have a different scout competing (unless the troop was too small, in which case some young men would do several of the events). At the end of the evening of Olympian events, the Scout Master Splash would be the final point-gathering opportunity for each team.

The Scout Master Splash, though, belonged to the adult leaders. That year there was some question as to which of the dads would do this part of our troop's event. Our exceptionally worthy Scout Master had a bad back and was thin, so he wasn't going to participate. There were a couple guys who fit the girth necessary, but ... when the boys started asking me to do it (back in the days in which my girth was less visible), I figured I'd have to add a little something to this event. There was no way that my frame was going to create the splash needed for bigger points, so *style* would be required.

What can I say? It lacked *life*; it had no gusto (though it had plenty of gut). It was... quiet...and lame.

So, that year, as Troop 146 looked on, as well as the eyes of all the other troops and their well-rounded scout leaders, I stepped to the side of the pool, dramatically put my arms straight out, leapt high into the air, and performed one of the most reddening belly flops of my life.

I came out of the water to find that, not only was the entirety of the front of my body red, but the dive had gone over rather well. The cheering was loud and long, the other scout leaders were rather congratulatory, and the event seemed to have swung the way of Troop 146.

After that year there was never another year in which several scout leaders did not perform with more enthusiasm, more zest, more passion. The camp judges began to bring a large measuring stick by which they would estimate splash height, they would sometimes become participants in the whole show, even as they provided judging. Men would jump into the pool in full scout uniform, belly flops became a norm, other outfits came into play, and there was more *show* put into the entire event than I'd seen in all prior years.

Did I do that? I doubt it. Chances are there was more showmanship in other weeks of scout camp (there were six weeks every summer) and we just didn't see it. Our troop was always more competitively driven, and the momentum of the boys didn't really change. They did seem to look forward to that part of the evening more than previously, but... who knows.

Anyway, *that* became a norm for our troop. I may never do a belly flop elsewhere for the entire year, but when it came time for the big show at camp, *I was in my element*.

But, in this year... something else was going on. Another new thing was in development.

You have to understand. I had been coming to this camp for a week every year from a hard, time-consuming, life-consuming job. As an operations manager at our numbers-driven company, I would arrive at the camp *needing* time away. Time lying in a tent in the woods was perfect. Restful, refreshing, invigorating, quiet at all the right times ... everything I wanted and needed. My wife always *wanted* me to go to camp. At the end of the week, she knew that I was "in camp mode"—which was to say, *alive, ready, active* ... just... fully awake and alive again. I don't know how else to describe it.

That week at camp every year would *reinvigorate* me.

In fact, a short story about just how much it reinvigorated me. I was always a fairly active guy—loved playing sports, doing physical things out-of-doors. But I never really had much physical strength. I had beaten some boys and men who were stronger than me in some things—arm wrestling, high jump, foot races, whatever—but my strength was more of *tenacity* than anything else. One day, while my oldest son was taking a climbing course in the farther back woods of the campground, a few friends and I walked out to visit the class. During a lull in the boys' action, I asked the merit badge counselor if I could try climbing the firecracker rope ladder that was hanging there, unused. He was game.

They hooked me up with the climbing gear (regulations are regulations), and I began climbing the firecracker ladder. I grabbed as high up as I could, then got my two feet to come together around the rope, on top of a lower rung. I kept inching up the ladder—one pair of rungs at a time. I'd move my hands up another set, and then pull my feet up until I could get them to agree on the next rung, surrounding the rope. One after another, I struggled to the top. Everyone on the ground just kept watching, not moving on to other activities. I stopped for a moment of breathing at least once. Then, back to work, I'd reach up for another rung, grab it with both hands, and struggle to pull myself up enough to get my feet on a rung another level higher.

In the end, I was on the platform above the firecracker ladder, being congratulated.

The young man in charge of the course said something that rattled me.

"I've been here for many years. Nobody has ever done that before."

I found that hard to believe. Again, I had never been a physically strong man, or a physically strong boy. Apparently, though, in my Boy-Scout-Camp-Mode, or somewhere along the way in my personal tenacity, I had accomplished something.

Where was I? Oh, yes, the Tarzan Yell.

Early in this particular week, already feeling the *life* surging through my limbs and heart, I began doing something a little... unusual.

The Tarzan Yell.

Yeah, right there in our campground. In fact, early in the morning. It was just my way of saying, "Good Morning!" to the creatures and scouts of the world. I would suck in a big breath of air, look upward, and just let it rip. It was clunky, oft scratchy, not the perfect shout of the 'real Tarzan', but... it worked, and it became a troop regular.

If it was time for the boys to get up, and movement hadn't been as existent as it ought, I would offer a little help.

Some of the boys, those who really ought to have been more mobile at that point of the morning, would actually get to hear the Tarzan yell inside their tents—as I would open the flap just enough, put my mouth in, suck in a deep breath, and let it rip. Sometimes the boys knew it was coming and would shout out, "We're up! We're up!" Activity happened.

Sometimes, the boys just needed a good wake up call.

Um... smiley face.

The Tarzan Yell picked up momentum. Like orange juice, it wasn't just for breakfast anymore. Periodically throughout the day I would stand up, suck in a big breath, and let the world know that I was fully alive.

Somewhere around Wednesday a few of us dads were sitting back at camp chatting (or, perhaps, napping) while the boys were finishing up merit badge classes for the day. We heard a weak yell somewhere in the distance. One of the dads perked up, realizing what was going on.

He said, "I think they're calling you."

We listened more intently. Sure enough—it was a novice Tarzan Yell. Well, it seemed the younger monkeys were itching to join the world of gorillas.

I stood up, sucked in a good breath, and let 'er rip.

And that, my friends, continued throughout the week. It got to the point where it might happen anytime, anywhere on campus.

We might be walking down our trail, Tarzan Yell. Walking through the main grounds, Tarzan Yell. I'd let one rip while we were walking to the campfires, and, inevitably, would hear responses from a variety of directions.

Anywhere.

Anytime.

So... as you can see, it became a habit. It had become almost like... breathing.

So ...

On Thursdays, one of my buddies and I would go into town to pick up more supplies. Our troop was a 'self-sufficient' troop—that is, we did all of our own cooking and cleaning up. So, we wouldn't take all the meat and veggies and fruits that we were going to eat for the week when we first drove in, but would have to re-supply during the week at a nearby town's grocery stores. This reminds me—remind me to tell you about the time that we picked up soy burgers to save money. Ick.

Anyway, there I stood in the breakfast cereal aisle. My buddy was several feet down the aisle, behind me.

I turned, looked at the cereal, took a deep breath, and...

Oh. My. Gosh. I looked over at my buddy, my mouth still open, my eyes wide with shock. His eyes went wide. He turned the cart and nearly sprinted out of the aisle.

And... I realized just how close I had come.

Holy smokes.

That was too close.

Conversation

My hand was already on the door handle.

"Anything special going on this weekend?"

It wasn't quite a normal question. Something felt, to me, like he actually meant it. It wasn't the customary, "What's up?" greeting one of his peers gave me umpteen times per day. It wasn't the "Mr. Cheatwood!" or "How you doin'?" that was said to me so many times, every single day, that I had given up answering the questions—finally succumbing to how such things were used as just another way of saying, "Hello". I had finally given in to these meaningless greetings. Every time I heard such things now I either didn't bother responding with anything more than a hand wave, or responded with my own miniscule "Hey there".

No, this wasn't a meaningless question. Something about this question was *real*.

I took my hand off of the door handle. Pulling my shoulder off the door, where I had already leaned in to make my escape, something was going on at a million miles per hour somewhere inside, but I desperately wanted to slow it all down.

For a moment.

He had turned his chair towards me as he asked the question. I stepped around to face him.

We talked about my daughter being home from school. About her up-coming flight to Florida. We talked about the fact that she hadn't been free to make our family's annual trip to Florida for the last four years while she had been in college. I told him about the fact that my wife's parents were paying to have our daughter fly to Florida during her Spring break to visit them on their lengthy vacation. We talked about his recent trip to Florida. He told of the house he and his wife were looking at down there, the fact that they were considering buying something that was on stilts. We both laughed about that.

We talked about our company's buy-out program, his willingness to sign such a deal and leave, his lack of having received one. We talked about my having received an offer to do so, my inability or unwillingness to sign it and leave. He talked about how he didn't think anybody who wasn't close to retirement age would feel free to take the severance offer and run, because jobs were so hard to come by.

He had set aside what he had been working on—signatures needed, numbers to decipher, corrections to be made. I had sat down in a chair opposite him. We were having a real talk between two real men who had two very real lives.

We were *conversing*.

We both listened to the other, not needing to run our words over those of the other, not having our own agenda to carry in the conversation. We heard, we spoke, and we appreciated the moment.

And it was very good.

I had known this man for many years—more than the years I had known anyone else in the local management group. Prior to taking a manager job myself, I had talked with him on the phone. I'd called from Arkansas as I was considering the possibility of taking a courier job he had offered in our job system. In the end, I chose not to do so, because my moving expenses would be my own to pay. Instead, I waited to become a manager, got my moving expenses paid, and, in time, ended up being one of his peers at two different stations.

And here we were—slowing down, talking about our lives, and not being too busy to hear. I am ashamed to notice how rare this is.

A while back I had made "listening" a "word-of-the-year" for myself. That had gone pretty well, honestly. I had put listening skills into action far more during that year, and I think those skills have continued. As a father of six children, and a long time husband of one wonderful woman, I ought to be a very good listener. But, my listening skills can always use some improvement. Can one really have too much listening? My intent that year was to do more listening with family and friends. I did do more, but, as I said, can you really have too much?

Our conversation was healthy, wholesome, real, and ... restful. It was friendship. It was not business.

There we sat, treating each other as something other than a something, other than a number, an appointment, an agenda. We *genuinely* heard each other. We didn't check our cell phones, didn't take any phone calls, didn't answer any emails. We did not run over each other's words with our own. We did not have something we had to say so very desperately that we were willing to shove it into the sentences of the other man in the conversation. We did not have something we had to say that we deemed important enough to interrupt—that we thought was more important than what the other guy said.

And... it was good.

He's Eleven

He's eleven.

That thought slipped by the bottom of the screen of my mind as I stood outside the garden shed, gazing across the yard at William. On the other side of the yard, along the western edge of our property, he was swinging an old scythe through high grass.

Swoosh, swoosh, swoosh.

There was something about this scene that I wanted to keep. I stood still, trying to be stuck in this exact moment, but wondering how much time I would have to enjoy scenes just like this one. Yes, there would be other children to watch, but they wouldn't be this one. They may be a generation removed from his generation. They may be his children. Yes, I'll take pleasure in watching grand children as they grow, but... I imagine there will never be anything quite like watching my William. Or Silas. Or any of our own. Seeing him freely swinging through the weeds, seeing the pleasure that he was taking in it ... How can Heaven not be like this?

How can Heaven not be *just... like... this*?

I wanted to stand there and take it all in. To drink in every moment of *this* that I could grab. Forever. His pleasure was obvious. Nobody told him to do this. Nobody asked. Something in this little boy's heart compelled him to pick up this boy-sized tool and take up this man's work.

Maybe it wouldn't last for long. Maybe the tool would be too dull to give the real satisfaction that comes with work accomplished. Maybe he would do several feet of weed hacking, look up, see dozens of yards to go, and have the wind taken out of his sails. Maybe discouragement would set in, so quick and deep, that the joy of what he was doing would be overwhelmed, forgotten, and discarded.

Swoosh, swoosh, swoosh.

My mind took pictures. Lord, let these pictures stay freshly available in my heart.

I stood there watching, wondering how long this would last. How long could I watch before he would notice? If he noticed, would he quit? Would this bashful young child quit because he discovered he had an audience? Might I ruin the wonder of his work? Of this ... art?

I didn't want to ruin it. But my heart craved moments like this.

Swoosh, swoosh, swoosh.

I took my hand out of my pocket. If he were to suddenly look up and see me watching, I wanted to be able to quickly give a thumbs-up sign—a quick acknowledgement from Dad of a job well done. That might be just the thing it would take to encourage him to stay the course, to keep at it.

Swoosh, swoosh, swoosh.

Old pictures began to spring out of the files of my mind. A young Joseph, charging ahead on a hiking trail. Red, bobbing curls on the small head of a bright-eyed and crafting Elise. The constant smile of a towhead named Ian. The hands of a young boy named Sean, holding tools as he so often did. Silas in a suit and tie, preparing for a public speech at the age of seven.

Every child unique. Every picture precious.

I stood, watching.

Swoosh, swoosh, swoosh.

For more than two hours I had been working in the yard and field. Weeds on a fence row had fallen. That fence row always took more trimmer string, because it was hard to cut the grass without having the string lost against that hard wire, chopping off trimming string before its time. The high weeds now lie on the ground under that fence. They lie there waiting for the wind to spread them, stray chickens to scatter them in their search for food, or the mower to make them nearly invisible, like the tiny pieces of trimmer string that were spent to cut them down.

On this day, the fence and post had been reclaimed.

The grass that sought to claim the concrete behind the barn lost yet another battle, beaten back to its intended boundaries. In front of the bank barn, older concrete, laid there by strangers long before we arrived on the scene, was freely breathing air again, taking in the sunshine. The word "dominion" came to mind every time I cleaned up that area.

Years earlier, a brief conversation with a good, hard-working young man about the grass and that concrete:

"Mr. C., why don't you just let the grass cover it?"

"Because it doesn't belong there."

"But it takes a lot of work to knock that back all the time."

"Adam, this is just one small way in which I am practicing dominion."

As I finished trimming back that grass earlier, I stepped back from my work and said, "I win."

I had won the battle.

I love that battle. In the long run, I will lose it. One day I will quit cutting that grass back from my old concrete. One day I will either die, or sell the property, or be so pained and crusty and bent that I can no longer keep up that fight. Maybe one of the kids will continue the fight. Maybe a stranger. Maybe someone will finally decide to tear out the concrete, or replace it, or just let the grass win.

But, in the meanwhile, I still stood above that reclaimed concrete and cherished the victory. Happy to see the well-outlined old concrete showing its face to the sun, the grass tamed once again.

For me, that was absolute pleasure.

Let me touch the grass
Walk through the field
Let me take back the concrete
From the natural growth
Of the grass that surrounds it

Let me run a mower
A weed whacker
Let me clip away brush
And bothersome tree starts

Let me stop the acts of nature
Which aim to overtake my land
Attempting to *be* the master

Let me live in this domain
Practicing dominion
Over this small plot of land
Let me pull weeds
With these aging fingers
Though they may hurt
For hours afterward

Let me take those sore fingers
And sit on the floor
Of my living room
Rubbing my wife's tired feet

How are these things not Heavenly? How much better can a life get?

Swoosh, swoosh, swoosh.

I stood watching William. There is poetry in a young boy playfully swinging a scythe at high weeds. Playfully, yet doing real work. Just like his dad. I stood there, barefoot, grass shards covering my bare shins, specks of grass sprinkled all over my clothes and arms—remnants of battle. Of battle won. My feet had no grass covering, thanks to pools of water leftover from the rains that rinsed my feet as I walked.

My dominion work continues. This child aims to take part of that work. He will rise up, take the scythe, and do battle. Like his father.

Right now, he's only eleven.

Swoosh, swoosh, swoosh.

Reminder Bridge

I work about 20 miles from home. Unless, of course, I take a bike ride to get to there. Then I work 22.5 miles from home.

But what a glorious 22.5 miles it is.

May I say, first of all, that I absolutely love riding my bike to and from the office. I just wanted to point that out. I've done it quite a few times the last couple summers, and it has been wonderful. When I do make that bike ride, I roll over a wooden bridge on the south side of Troy. One morning, a couple things occurred to me as I did so.

First of all, I loved the fact that some thoughts would turn out to be associated with places, or smells, or other senses—and that those same thoughts would re-surface when you pass those same places, hear those same sounds, smell those same odors. For example, I still remember listening to the story of Corrie ten Boom while I was weeding one specific part of the garden. Each time I am weeding that area, I am reminded of the part of her story in which her sister is dying in prison. Sad part of the story, yes, but *it is rich*.

I was reminded of that concept that morning, though, because that bridge had drawn a consistent thought from my mind.

Secondly, that thought. The bridge has boards running lengthwise from one end to the other. Those boards are about six inches wide. Almost every time I ride on the bridge I aim to stay on *one* board all the way across (which is 25 to 30 yards). If I look down in front of me in hopes of staying on a single board,

I fail badly. However, if I look *ahead,* keeping my eyes on the distant end of the bridge, I am far more likely to stay on one board all the way across the bridge.

This little fact of nature reminds me of something significant about many of my hopes, dreams, and ambitions. I often think that I have few such things, but am then reminded of the enormity of *real* aims that I have in my simple, normal life. I'm a husband, a father, a brother, an employee, a friend, an uncle, a nephew, a deacon, etc. All of these things come with some responsibility, or, at the very least, there are things to *do* inside of each that makes one *good* at them.

The bridge reminds me that the best way to stay 'on track' in fulfilling those life purposes it to look ahead, at the goal in mind, rather than looking directly down at the individual footsteps I am taking. Clearly, those footsteps are important, but to focus on them is to lose sight of the goal. And, as happens on that bridge, when I lose sight of the goal I stray from it.

So, that bridge is a good reminder to me. I need to get some of those larger visions back in my sites and stop looking down at my feet.

2 A.M. Gratitude

At the end of a long day of car shopping, which was interspersed with sneezing fits, I crashed into bed around 10:00, physically drained. I don't know what happened at 10:05, because I was GONE.

However, around 1 AM I found myself awake. Increasingly, of late, I have made an effort to turn such moments into times of thanksgiving prayers. It is a practice I have come to identify as helpful in pulling my selfish heart out of depression.

As I told the Lord of my thankfulness for various people in my life that early morning, it occurred to me that I could use some Thank You cards to encourage some of those same people with words of gratitude.

Hmm. I don't have any Thank You notes...

But, at 1:30 in the morning, Walmart does!

Quietly, I got out of bed, pulled some clothing out of my closet, and left the bedroom. At my desk, I got dressed, put on my glasses, hat, and shoes, grabbed wallet and keys ...and was on my way to Wally World at a preposterous time of "day."

I was in no hurry. A leisurely drive into town revealed the fact that several pairs of folks were out walking shortly before 2:00 AM in Troy. Their clothing didn't indicate exercise, but that their night out was coming to its quiet close.

A train.

Another pair of walkers.

A few cars between me and the store.

Park the van, make sure the wallet is in my coat, walk in.

Again, I'm in no hurry. I walk through the store wondering whether little Christmas gifts will jump off the shelves and get my attention. A coffee cup has my fingerprints, but remains without fulfilled purpose; a bag of tools was considered for an industrious son; bags of chocolate could be purchased later; the jewelry counter was closed for the night...

Where are the cards? Ah, there they are.

I didn't really want individual cards, but a mass of them. I didn't feel the need to buy fancy, but a Thank You Card that could look like it was from a man. I settled on a box of fairly plain Thank You notes... The words I would write in them would be the point anyway.

One available register, brief chatter with lady, head to the van.

Saturday, while I was out hunting for a car in our other vehicle, Angel had been out with the van. She had texted me that it was sluggish to start. That wasn't surprising to me—it had been odd about starting ever since we bought it. The battery had suffered from young boys leaving a door open overnight, internal lights being left on for days, and a glove box light that wasn't always *obviously* on. Inevitably, we'd get it all running again, though sometimes it would require a jump.

Like tonight.

At 2 AM.

At Walmart.

I sat there for a moment after hearing the dull silence of a battery in open rebellion. 2 AM, I thought. What interesting timing.

"Father, how about a nudge?" I prayed. He had given nudges on behalf of this van on previous occasions.

Turn the key. Silence—more than before. Or... would that be called 'less?'

"Right."

Sometimes when the van acts like this, it'll turn over normally a few moments later. I gave it a few minutes, sitting quietly and calmly in the van. My mind did that little "accessing" thing while I waited—trying to dig out a contingency plan.

Turn key.

Silence. And I do not mean the golden kind.

I checked the back of the van for jumper cables, though I was sure I'd left them in the truck.

I had.

Closing the door, I had one of those moments of abnormal clarity—the kind when you can clearly identify the temptation the enemy is lying before you. I was tempted to say something ugly to my van. Instead, I quietly said, "You failed me *this time*."

It was a conscious recognition of many thousands of miles of faithfulness. Later, I remembered it, too, as a moment of real gratitude.

Walmart sells jumper cables. Even at 2 AM. I walked back in, muddled around again, found some options, considered them, and went cheap. I've never had a cheap pair of jumper cables fail me.

Of course, the lady at the register recognized me. We talked for a moment about why I was back.

"Do you have someone to help you jump the battery?"

"No."

She humorously suggested opening the hood and looking pathetic. I told her that look came somewhat naturally to me, so I might try it.

FYI—there aren't a whole lot of people in the parking lot of Walmart at 2:00 AM.

Still, I managed to get assistance from an employee who was sitting in her SUV during a break. Battery charged, I thanked her, and she went back to work.

I drove home, formulated a small plan to get the battery checked the next day, and gave thanks. I thanked God that it happened to me, rather than my wife; that someone was available to help me; that it happened in the right parking lot; etc.

Out of the van, between it and the house, I was struck by the brightness of the moonlit sky. Out here, in the country, we can see the stars far better than in a Walmart parking lot. As I stood staring into the sky, I remembered the simple and wonderful truth that God said, "Let there be light," then created the sun, moon, and stars ... a couple days later.

Clearly, our source of Light is not found even in a beautiful sky.

I walked into my home grateful, and with a handful of Thank You notes.

If you have been blessed with the often absurd gift of parenthood, you probably are well aware that every child is different than the others. My wife and I have a ridiculous assortment. There's one, though, who I have often referred to as our 'cartoon character.'

Sean, the Choke Artist

He was 11 at the time. Going on 31 some days, 17 others ... and six the remainder.

One day he and Ian rode with another one of the Boy Scout dads to a merit badge course down south of Dayton. Angie had given them coupons for Burger King—buy a meal, get a sandwich free. The idea was that they would share the coupons with their buddies, eat normal, blah blah blah.

So... the other night Angie comes into the living room to tell me something. She's laughing. She begins to tell me about something that had happened, but Sean ...

- rushes into the living room,
- begins slapping her on the back,
- holds his hand over her mouth,
- looks at me,
- and shouts, "She's choking!"

I bust a gut.

Obviously, he didn't want me to hear what she was about to tell me.

So, as funny as what Sean was doing to his mother was, the rest of the story pales... but here it is. Turns out, Ian and Sean took the coupons, used one each, and both consumed two Big Macs, large Cokes, large fries... and spent about fourteen bucks on lunch that day. Apparently they hadn't quite caught the 'how to save money with a coupon' concept.

We may never have known about this, except for my wonderful wife, who asks good questions... and who found out that they owed a few bucks to one of the Scout dads.

And, perhaps, I can say the 'cartoon character' comes by it honestly.

Laughing at the Dentist

As a boy I never had a dentist appointment at which the dentist said those magical words, "No cavities."

Ever.

My older brother, Dennis, was always getting those remarkable words spoken in his presence... that's the only reason I even knew such a phrase existed.

Reason? I don't know, but I speculate:

- I got G-Pa Macy teeth, Dennis got G-Pa Cheatwood teeth
- I was a sweet-tooth kind of kid, Dennis was a milk lover

Somewhere in there, the truth exists. It wasn't too many years ago, though, when a dentist said to me, "No cavities". I was incredulous for a moment.

"What did you say?"

"No cavities."

I laughed at him. "Right," I said, "very funny. So, what's going on in there?"

But... he meant it.

Due to my lifelong cavity problems, I had a head full of fillings before I was in high school. Those fillings, the old silver kind, had begun to have problems. I guess they lose their seal or something in the long run.

One morning I had one of those fillings dealt with. I had been in to see the dentist too often at the time. A few months earlier I had a tooth fall out of my head while I sat at a soccer game. No, I hadn't been hit in the head with a ball. Nope, wasn't chewing gum. I was picking something from between two teeth when the thing simply cracked off and fell out.

I was stunned. Immediately I thought through what might have happened to cause it, but I came up with no excuses, no ideas. I decided that my Macy teeth were kicking it up a notch. None of this 'no cavities' nonsense for them, no! Or, my elderliness (I was 43 at the time) was activating, and that my whole head of teeth would be gone in a matter of months.

I'm not paranoid, so stop thinking that!

Alas, no. The dentist said that was the tooth I'd had a root canal on several years earlier and that it wasn't uncommon for such teeth to break off eventually. So, my top far-left tooth is gone (and, for a right-winger like me, that's quite fitting).

A couple weeks later I was done eating dinner when I noticed a gaping hole in a tooth. Aaugh! I tried to remember what had happened. We had been eating hamburger, but I thought I'd hit one of those itsy bones that sometimes show up. Maybe that little thing I hit wasn't a beef bone, but my chipped tooth.

After I told the dentist to just take me out back and shoot me, he said it was a filling that had fallen out. He re-filled it, and on I went.

But, they had taken X-rays. One of the pictures showed some decay under yet another filling. The appointment was made. Then, at that appointment, I sat in the chair, he laid me back, lowered me most of the way to the floor, grabbed a needle device, and pricked my gums. Things began going numb.

"If I come in here any more often, I'll have to start paying rent," I said.

He laughed. I laid there thinking about what I had just said.

"I guess I *am* paying rent."

He, evil fiend that he was, laughed again. But, at least it wasn't a maniacal laugh.

Drilling.

I'm an old hand at this, so it doesn't bother me much. He cleaned out the area, I smelled burning tooth, etc. He was about done when he stuck another instrument in there and...

Grunk grunk grunk grunk!!

When he was done, I said, "Are you landing an airplane in there?"

A while later he used it again. I chuckled again... even had a little bit of a belly laugh going. That sound in my head was simply too thunderous to *not* be funny to me. This time, though, I knew exactly what it sounded like.

"I know what that is! It is those ridges at the side of the highway! You keep driving on them!"

He said, "That's exactly right!"

I like my dentist. He laughs at my jokes. I like getting people to laugh.

I can't help thinking, though, whether he may have been just a little concerned when this guy who had been in his chair four times in a short period of time (and I go back again next Wednesday) was losing it. Surely he hadn't encountered belly laughs while drilling...

A Sad Restaurant, but....

I whispered to Ian, "This will be our last time here, I think."

He whispered, "The first, and the last!" His eyes were bright and cheery as he said it.

The waitress had just seated us at a booth that looked normal enough—napkins holding our silverware, salt and pepper available, clean table top. We had looked around the room upon entering only to find that there was only one other patron. He looked like a hobo off the street. Leaning over his meal, he grunted at the waitress when she walked by him asking whether everything was okay. Apparently she understood the language.

Something about the place subdued us. We didn't talk aloud during most of our stay. The music, although pleasant Christmas music, was playing so low that you felt compelled to keep silent. And they weren't playing "Silent Night".

I had found the place through using our coupon book—you know the kind, they often have restaurants in them that can't quite get enough business on their own, or new restaurants looking to get started. You don't often find the really good restaurants in those things, although there are exceptions. This place *needed* the endorsement of a coupon book.

Earlier I had dropped Ian at a class and headed out to check out a list of potential restaurants from our little book. The first restaurant I checked out was now boarded up. As I drove by this one, I couldn't quite make out whether it was open. The big sign out front was not lit, unlike most of the restaurants nearby. The sign was also rather warped—as though it had been there for quite some time, or had stood too close to a fire.

I had to drive into the driveway and go slowly past the front door in order to figure out whether they were still in business.

Ah! The "open" sign was lit, and so tiny that one had to look very closely. Sure seemed like they were trying to hide the sign, though. Or, at least, they weren't putting it in the most useful and helpful place. Well, it was open, so I'd bring Ian back here during his break in debate class.

When we returned, the big sign still wasn't lit up, even though the darkness was settling in for the evening. We parked the car close to the front—wherever we wanted to, really, because there were only a couple cars in the lot. A lack of automobiles in the lot is often a warning to us about restaurants, no?

Ian and I got out of the car and walked slowly toward the front door. As we opened it, I looked straight forward to find a restaurant-like front desk, cluttered with a few papers, a clipboard, and a copier – fax machine. No cash register.

What drew my attention, though, was the cranky-looking older woman to the left. She was sitting at a very messy desk, hunched over some papers. She did not look up as we entered, didn't greet us, and kept at her work. By the look of her, I'd have thought she was an auditor going over the restaurants receipts, and that she was not pleased.

As we approached the front desk, the angry-looking, short, old woman shuffled around and headed that direction, but not for us. Never even gave us eye contact. She was getting something off the desk, totally ignoring us customers. The hostess finally appeared, looking about as subdued as the place felt. I don't know about Ian, but I felt like I had to be somewhat quiet from the start.

So, here we were at our booth, looking over the menus. The hostess then became our waitress, asking whether we'd like something to drink. Helpfully, she explained that they had Pepsi products, and a few other things. We both went for the pink lemonade. How can somebody have Pepsi products but not carry Mountain Dew?

Then, as she took a leisurely stroll away from us, we both looked at each other in silent astonishment. Perhaps Ian was thinking like I was.

"Seriously? Do we want to eat here?"

Well... we had a buy one get one free, so... yes.

"Once."

"Yes, only once."

We looked over the menus. Prices seemed normal enough; it had a good selection, and a pretty wide variety.

Having made my selection (lasagna—surely they can't mess that up, right?), I looked around the restaurant for a moment. The salad bar was a monstrosity in the middle of the dining hall. A big, silver, fairly well-lit island that appeared right out of "utilitarian restaurant items" magazine. Sitting on wheels, it looked like they might wheel it away whenever they were done with it. The walls were a dark mustard-like color, but not appalling. Could be seen as 70s, but could be somewhat modern. The far wall had that interesting look of plaster broken off of under-lying brick. Not bad. Not *too* bad.

I looked out our window, gazing at the warped, old-looking sign. Perhaps the lights, which still weren't on, had warped the sign? Maybe it was cheap plastic. Whatever it was, it didn't look very inviting.

So…. What was it that compelled us to talk so silently? Was it the low-volume music? Something here was… subduing.

The waitress came back to visit. Ian ordered, I ordered, and she said my meal came with a salad bar. As she walked away, Ian leaned towards me and said, in very low tones, "She talks like she's falling asleep. Even her eyelids seem ready to go."

"Maybe she is," I said. "Sure seems forcefully quiet here."

I got up to get my salad.

When I stood at the salad bar, I saw six things: iceberg lettuce, some yellow goopy-looking stuff with something lumpy in it, two puddings, maybe cottage cheese, and those tiny reddish bacon bit things.

No salad dressing.

Seriously?? I wondered how this got called a salad bar. Nevertheless, I began to put some iceberg lettuce on my plate. As I passed the other items, I came upon a second, lower platform of items—which were not in the over-powering light, but in shadow. Ah! I found black olives, pickles, cucumbers, etc. Whew, I thought, options. And, happily, salad dressings.

I built my salad and returned to our booth.

First thing I tried was the black olives. Uh oh, I thought, this could be rough. They were not very fresh. I'd tasted better black olives out of a can, in fact.

I ate. We talked about little things. In a little way. In little voices.

Our meals came. The portion sizes were impressive. My lasagna appeared to be two meals (and it became two, as I chose to eat half and save the other half for work the next day). Ian's Philly cheesesteak sandwich was large and good-looking. He didn't eat it all! That was somewhat shocking to me. This was a young man who ate like a horse.

Then, the trouble started—I began thinking.

The waitress came back to visit. Yes, things were good. In an effort to bring some light to her otherwise dreary-seeming existence, I tried to engage her in some conversation. We talked about the restaurant. It had been there only since May—about six months. I asked her about the name (which had a "ll" in it), digging for any significance. Sure enough, it was a second restaurant. She described where the other place was, and then left us to enjoy our food.

"Ian," I said, "you know how we talk about our purpose being to glorify God and enjoy Him forever?"

He nodded assent.

"Okay, let's say that you are an employee here. What can you do?"

We looked around the restaurant and thought a bit.

It's not necessarily easy to do, but I think it's important. We are given a purpose here, and I like to think of that purpose in the terms of that catechism point—What is the chief end of man? The chief end of man is to glorify God and to enjoy Him forever.

Good stuff.

We talked together about what such a thing might look like at a restaurant. How might we, playing the role of 'the waiter,' bring God glory in such a place? It seemed like the atmosphere was the main issue. The food was actually pretty good, portions a great take-home size, décor wasn't bad. That initial experience—both outside and at the front door—did leave something to be desired, but that may be beyond our reach as the "waiter," so we left it alone.

What would we want done? We would want our customers to feel comfortable, to enjoy their food, to feel like they can talk with each other freely and enjoyably, that they are even free to laugh out loud. We'd want the tables clean, orderly, and ready for the next customer. We'd want salt and pepper filled and ready.

The list goes on. What we thought about this particular restaurant, though, was that the atmosphere itself was extinguishing the joys of the sought-after restaurant experience. As a "waiter," we may not have much to say about that, but we thought a few things would be within our reach.

1. Turn the music up. If nobody got in our way we'd turn it up a bit, because we thought the exceedingly low music was a part of the problem. It seemed to urge us to keep quiet—the kind of quiet that may as well just shut up and eat. Two other tables of patrons came in while we were there, and we noticed that they ate their meals with similar quietude. Yes, turn up the music. It was good music, so that shouldn't be a problem. Don't turn it up so loud that conversation is difficult.

2. Ourselves. Everyone has probably had very positive experiences with a waiter or waitress—someone who made you glad to be at the restaurant you selected for a given meal. A good waiter or waitress can make up for mediocre food. Yes, we decided, we needed to be a little gregarious, playful, even teasing. Of course, that doesn't work for everybody, but a good waiter or waitress can read folks well enough to know just what kind of jocularity or calm-kindness to bring to the table. That would be necessary, and pleasing to God.

3. Serve well. Observe patrons closely, understanding what they need and when they need it. Don't be annoyingly service-oriented—that is, don't bother folks so much that you hinder their ability to have free-flowing conversation at the table. Again, this is going to differ from patron to patron. Figure it out, practice it, use it.

4. Anything else we could persuade the owners/managers to do—like hide that hideous table, move the cranky lady to the back of the restaurant, etc.

The conversation was well worth having. It's so important that we teach our children about our basic reason for living— bringing glory to God, and primarily doing so through the love we work out towards those around us. We want our kids thinking about how they can do so in any field of work, in any endeavor. They need to be thinking about what *serving* looks like, what it means to bear one another's burdens, what it looks like to actively love our neighbor, and the like.

Recently I read about Eric Lidell, the Olympic runner portrayed in the movie Chariots of Fire. His father once said to him, "Eric, you can praise the Lord by peeling a spud if you peel it to perfection. Don't compromise. Compromise is a language of the devil. Run in God's name, and let the world stand back in wonder."

That, my friend, is good stuff.

An Eight Year Old Hand

An eight year old hand
Rested on my chest
Above a formerly stone heart
It had been softened
Along the way
This crusty heart of mine
As evidenced
By his unconscious willingness
To lie there
In that embrace

He starts each night
In his own bed
But sometimes ends up in ours
Not for reasons,
I think,
Of fear or dread
But for love

When I am awake
In the middle of the night
I, too, will lie there
With my Father

Baseball, Fatherhood, and Sonship

A boy sits on the stairs, holding ten packages of baseball cards close to his chest. The money he had used had been his own. But... a rule had been broken. He had tried to hide them on his way up the steps, but his dad had caught him, as though he had been hunting. Perhaps the boy had looked too suspicious as he hurried into the house. There would be a price to pay, and it would not be in cash.

He loved baseball. The numbers meant something to him. They were like music in his ears. Yes, the numbers sang to him. He could spend *hours* looking at baseball cards, one at a time, not even trying to memorize the statistics of good and bad players alike, but memorizing them all the same. He knew the lifetime statistics of players whose names he would forget in the future. He knew the numbers of players who would be mostly forgotten by history itself. People like Gary Nolan, Rick Manning, Frank Duffy, and many other obscure players, would mean something to him whether they meant anything to anyone else or not. He would know what they had accomplished in their baseball careers. He even knew the height of Freddy Patek.

It was 1975, and Hank Aaron's card was important. The previous year he had hit the home run that broke the greatest record in sports. The record number of home runs in a career, in a lifetime, would be more than 714 for the very first time. The scene had played so often on the television that people who didn't even care about baseball at the time thought, years afterwards, that they had seen it live... when they hadn't.

The boy knew Al Downing's name, that was for sure. Yes, he had given up homerun number 715, but he wasn't a bad pitcher. He had his distinction now in baseball history. He deserved to be remembered for things he accomplished, rather than for this, but.. history is history.

Frank Robinson played for and managed the Cleveland Indians, the Big Red Machine was in full swing, Johnny Bench was amazing, Pete Rose hustled, Joe Morgan twitched, Nolan Ryan was just getting warmed up, and an eclectic group of players were playing for the boy's beloved Cleveland Indians.

But none of that mattered. Not in this moment.

The boy carries no memory of what happened next or before. The rule was that he could buy no more than two packages of baseball cards per week. Twenty cents, max. That was the rule. Each package carried ten cards and a stick of gum. The gum wasn't bad, but he mostly liked the smell of it. Sometimes that smell would linger on a card. The baseball cards, though... those were special things in the heart of the boy.

The more numbers, the better. It was great to see the stars of the game—young and old. But what he wanted was to see the multiple lines of statistics—and, preferably, the ones that didn't have a couple years of meaningless minor league numbers cluttering the view. Those were put there just to make themselves look more meaningful than they were. None of that nonsense.

He wanted more of the Hank Aaron type of cards—10, 16, 21 years of stats. He wanted to see lots of numbers in italics, indicating that the player led the league in that category that year. He wanted to see more guys with 200 or more hits in a season, 100 or more walks, less strike outs, high batting averages, 40 or more home runs, or 50+ stolen bases. He wanted to see pitchers with 20 or more wins, 300 or more strikeouts, low ERA...

The anger was... nonsensical. It was never easy to know just how angry he would make his dad. There wasn't a standard, a line, a ratio he could use to help him understand. The anger was unpredictable.

Oscar Gamble's card showed hair like nothing he had ever seen. And, of course, he was a Cleveland Indian. For the year.

Mike Schmidt's card was still young.

383 K's in a single year?! Nolan Ryan would always be a favorite.

On and on it went. The boy *loved* the numbers. The numbers of baseball. But... two per week was a number he neither understood, nor, on this day, obeyed.

How angry can a man get over a child buying ten packs of cards? And with his own money. A dollar.

Angry enough that the child only remembers the anger, nothing else. That whole moment is wrapped up in his mind with nothing more than a scene of him huddling on the steps, holding the dreaded ten, and knowing the reception of fury. Undefined, unpredictable, inexplicable fury.

Herb Washington. What a very odd idea, but what fun. In his ignorance, the boy did wonder whether he was related to his teammate, the more versatile Claudel Washington. No relation.

George and Ken Brett, though, were brothers. One a pitcher who could hit, the other a great and future Hall of Fame hitter. The boy would have his eye on George and his numbers for quite a few years, though he wasn't a Royals fan.

There were other brothers that year. The Niekros, for example. Alous, too.

The boy had brothers. But, typically, he played his baseball games alone. One brother may play catch in the backyard from time to time. A brother and a cousin would play 'hot box' on a Sunday afternoon. Maybe they'd shoot hoops, play a game of H.O.R.S.E. or P.I.G.

Joe Morgan. Bob Boone. Jeff Burroughs. Cesar Geronimo. Bill Matlock. Reggie Jackson. Vida Blue. Brooks Robinson. Darrell Evans. Gaylord Perry. Phil Niekro.

Don Baylor was beaned ten times that year—which was only half of the number that his teammate, Bobby Grich, endured.

Boog Powell (nope, not a typo) was an Oriole, but would soon become a much loved Cleveland Indian.

Andre Thornton was with the Cubs. It would be a couple more years before his glory years with the Cleveland Indians would begin.

No memory. Nothing beyond the steps, the ten packs, the rule that had been broken, and the white hot heat of irrational, out of balance, impenetrable and incomprehensible rage.

Rod Carew. Who could forget Rod Carew?

~ ~ ~

He threw the ball at the steps again, moved quickly to his right, and caught the ball. Sometimes the catcher didn't throw it back quite right. That was okay, because the boy could catch *anything*.

The whole time he threw and caught he was also talking out loud about a game that only he could see, only he could feel, only he could hear. The crowd, of course, was going wild. Or, in a different moment, they were perfectly quiet, in suspense. Or they were shouting, for good or for ill.

The pitcher, a boy wandering in his own field of dreams, was about to strike out the side in the bottom half of the ninth.

Great hitters played in that backyard. Pete Rose, Joe Morgan, Hank Aaron, Willie McCovey to name a few. Many great pitchers pitched against those concrete steps. None of them knew just how many pitches they threw, no batter knew how many swings he took. None of them knew that their hits rolled down a small hill into a backyard of wonder, that a boy ran down the hill and threw the ball back towards home plate in a vigorous attempt to catch them running too far. Hits that flew over his head might be doubles, but they might be outs if he chased them fast enough. If they hit the ball into the rock garden, the runners would freeze in time, in the air if necessary, between bases, as the boy would cautiously step on stones between flowers and other plants, in search of the ball.

Sometimes when a boy throws a ball, it doesn't do what the boy wants it to do.

In a related note—windows don't care much for baseball.

Oh. There went that one.

At this point, the boy had something to decide. Should he tell the truth about what happened and, eventually, suffer for telling the truth? Or, ought he to try to figure out a way to point the finger elsewhere? Or, even ignore it? It was a small window, a basement window. Just a crack.

Fear.

Fear had never been very far away from the boy. His bravest moments were all in fantasy. He cried on his first day of third grade, the first day in a strange land for this awkward boy from another town. That year he had stomach aches. Repeatedly. He missed school… on purpose. He hated going there. He didn't know people. People weren't nice.

Freckles frequently drew unwanted attention.

But, throwing a ball at the back steps of the house, he had the positive adoration of fifty thousand fans as he threw one fastball after another to hitters unsuspecting.

How did they never know it was coming?

He was capable. But *fear* compelled him to hide. Back seats in classrooms, the shortest and quickest route home, the quietest spots in the playground, the sidewalk less traveled, unencumbered by unknown kids who would likely tease him anyway…

He jumped up against the wall, caught the ball, and the fans went wild.

The boy had once read that Municipal Stadium had held over 100,000 fans for a World Series game. Though the Indians struggled to get to 20,000 during the dark years of these 70s, the bounds of his own imagination were outside of that little number.

The window. What to do about the window.

~ ~ ~

The boy stands at the kitchen sink, conversing with his dad. But now, many years later, they are in the boy's home. Gone are the days of throwing a ball against concrete steps. The boy has boys of his own.

The boy's father chokes up as he reminisces about their past. He says words that do not shock the boy—he already figured that they were true. But... there was shock in hearing his dad *admit*. There was something new, perhaps cathartic, in this... for both of them.

The conversation played in the boy's mind for many days.

Months.

Years.

In a way it troubled, but not nearly as much as it refreshed.

It reminded.

That day helped him to see something in his dad. Deep down, beneath the years, he saw that there was a young boy playing basketball somewhere by himself. No brothers, a busy father, a sister who had no interest in such things, this boy found pleasure in throwing a ball through a hoop. Such pleasure, in fact, that one of the most extraordinary and 'rebellious' acts of his young life would be breaking into a gymnasium at night in order to play basketball. It would be a story he would tell the boy many times.

His dad would have played, but he was busy. Busy creating a life for his family. Busy trying to make ends meet, busy trying to furnish their home, busy trying to bring happiness to a wife, busy… trying to meet the hidden expectations that his own father had inadvertently left in another young boy's aching, hungering heart. This story goes on for generations.

The boy and his father, standing at the kitchen sink, talk about the holes that fathers leave in the lives of sons. The mistakes, the… *humanity* that leaves us aching, dying, longing for more.

~ ~ ~

And the boy loves his dad.

They do not talk often…but the boy understands, as he grows older, that every father leaves pain in his wake. *Every* dad fails. He, too, had failed, was failing, and would fail again. He does not find this remarkable.

He has been told by some that he is a good dad… but he knows. He knows the failures that he has had, the ones that he is having … and he suspects some that are yet to come. He feels a similar *disconnect* with his own children, too frequently, and works to correct it. But there's only one real and lasting way to do so.

He warns his own sons of the pain that they will feel later in life, if they don't already feel it. He will fail them, he says. He will leave a hole in their hearts that only one Person can fill. He will leave a thirst, a hunger, a dying and desperate wish that only one Person can satisfy.

When he talks about Jesus with his sons, this is where he lands. This is the sticking point. This is the Redemption Story, the Great Escape, the Final Reckoning, the Inconceivable and Remarkable Ending to Every Story.

"...but whoever drinks the water that I give them will never thirst again..."

He talks about the sins of the fathers that are visited upon the children, about breaking the family curses, about fixing their eyes on Jesus, the author and perfecter of their faith. He tells them that they will not break those ugly bonds by wishing to, by focusing on what he did wrong in guiding them, or by fixating on his mistakes. They will break their own bonds by fixing their eyes on Jesus.

He tells them that every boy who grows up saying he won't be like his dad becomes... like his dad. The boy who grows into manhood by looking at Jesus, though, breaks the bonds, ends specific curses, and frees his future generations for something *greater*.

He tries to teach them not to spend their lives *reacting* to what he had been, the holes that he left. He tries to teach them to learn wisdom, to find out what is right and holy and true—and be those things.

~ ~ ~

The boy throws a ball.

A younger boy, who looks much like his dad, catches it.

I do not dance. However, one night, sometime well beyond our 25th year of marriage, we attended a wedding reception. This happened.

Last Night I Danced

Last night I danced
With the most beautiful woman in the world
They say we were at a reception
With four hundred people

I do not believe it
I swear to you
We were all alone

I saw no one
I heard no one
I felt no one

But her.

She tricked me into one dance
And taught my awkward frame
A little of how to move and lead

Friends quietly disappeared
Who, I think, had been nearby
Voices, like whispers in a dream, faded
And it was soon just she and I

She had sought me out
She had wanted this dance
But it was I who fell in love

We will dance again
Because there is Magic in it
And I will not let go

Produce, This is Mark

It was one of those mega-groceries. You know—a big chain store. You cannot throw a rock from one side to the other. Well… if you get a round rock, it might roll all the way to the other end. Hopefully you don't hit some sweet, old lady. Or the eggs. Yeah, don't hit the eggs.

Ya know what, just stop throwing rocks. Okay?

I was in the Produce section. My wife and I had just shaken down two pounds of water that was trying to escape via our lettuce. That wasn't happening. We've no interest in buying water we had no intention of drinking. How long have they been getting away with this—charging for lettuce by the pound, and having 'rules' that make them pour gallons of water on the stuff?

Whut.

At this point I was standing by the cart, not too far away from the lettuce. And water.

A phone rang.

I looked around for my wife—nowhere to be seen.

The phone rang again.

I looked around for it.

There it was—just a couple feet to the left of the lettuce. And water.

Ring ring.

Um… there's nobody around. I looked again to make sure my wife wasn't anywhere nearby. I didn't see her.

I can't help it. I'm afraid it's in my nature. I walked swiftly to the phone, picked it up, and said, "Produce, this is Mark."

Why in the world I was using my actual name, I cannot say.

"Hello, Mark, my name is Phyllis. I just need to know whether or not you have any more red grapes. The ones on sale."

"Hmm… just a minute. I'll check."

I gently set the phone down too near the lettuce, hoping that the lettuce would be considered wet-enough for just a moment. I walked over to where I hoped the grapes would be, but didn't find them. Uh oh. Where were they? Rushing over to the next table, I found them. I gave the table a glimpse, checked the price, the variety, the unit, etc.

Back to the phone.

"Ma'am?"

"Yes?"

"Yes, Ma'am, we have plenty of grapes left. They are currently 1.39 per pound. We also have some organic white grapes, but those are 2.99."

"Thank you very much."

"Glad to help! Have a great day!"

I hung up the phone and turned to hustle back to the cart, but saw my wife standing there staring at me.

"What are you doing?"

Caught! Augh!

"Someone needed to know whether we had any red grapes left."

I tried to say it nonchalantly, as though... well... that probably didn't turn out so well.

She tilted her head slightly one direction, nodded a bit, and went on with her shopping.

Whew.

I returned to the cart, to stand guard. You know how it is—you have to guard those things or somebody who has nothing better to do will take it away and put everything back—lettuce, remaining water, pickles, three gallons of milk, two pounds of cheese, cottage cheese, frozen pizzas, a single bag of chips (it was on sale), radishes, toilet paper, ... I'd been there long enough... didn't want that to happen.

Ring ring.

Uh oh.

Ring ring.

I looked around for my wife. Once again, she had evaporated.

Ring ring.

I moved *casually* over to the phone.

"Produce, this is Mark."

"Mark?"

"Yes, may I help you?"

There was a bit of a pause. For a while. I might have heard papers shuffling, as though somebody was trying to track down "Mark" on an employee list. Somewhere. In a hidden room. I got a little itchy…. Was there a security camera somewhere panning in my general direction? I gently set the receiver back and returned to my cart. Um… nonchalantly. Right?

Ring ring.

Oh boy.

Ring ring.

My wife came back to the cart. I was almost giddy. Perhaps I was having too much fun?

When at the grocery, wasn't I supposed to be nearly comatose? Wasn't that where I was supposed to be dragging my feet, pushing the cart, compliantly picking up extra cans of tomato sauce, etc?

But no… I was playing grocery store.

Ring ring.

She looked at me with a penetrating look.

Ring ring.

I grinned back at her, dumb as a rock.

"Why does that look make me nervous?"

"I have *no idea*," I lied.

Ring ring.

I didn't even look at the phone. I held her gaze. And she held mine.

Ring ring.

She smiled, and walked away.

"What fun!" I said, and rushed to the phone.

"Produce, this is Mark."

Why did I keep using my own name? This isn't illegal, right?

"Hello, do you have any white potatoes?"

"I'll check, Ma'am; can you hold?"

In addition to my dream of writing, if there was ever a sporting event in which I would enjoy 'going pro' (other than baseball, of course), it would be disc golf. Not a true golfer, I prefer the whizzing of a small disc through trees, over greens, and into oddly shaped baskets with chains. Fortunately, this is a sport love which, unlike my love for baseball, I have passed on to several of my kids. We all enjoy an afternoon of disc golf together from time to time.

However, this particular time, I was alone because I was away from home on travel.

Persistence and my favorite Golf Disc

Parking the car, I grabbed my iPod, opened the door, shut it, locked it, and began to walk towards the first 'hole' of the disc golf course that was three blocks from my hotel. This was going to be fun. It would also be a bigger challenge than the Troy course (which has a rather liberal 'par'), and a healthy walk (18 holes, rather than Troy's 9).

Podcast started in my ear, I stepped up to the concrete slab that was the launch spot, looked ahead to the long lane, tried to see where the disc golf basket was, hauled back, threw... and watched my longtime favorite golf disc, one I'd had for at least 15 years, float gently into the shallow woods well to the right of the throwing lane.

Whut.

~ ~ ~

Several years ago we had a family reunion—Mom, Dad, my brothers and their families, me and mine. There's a Christian camp some friends own and operate about thirty minutes from my house, and we chose that as the site of this particular get together. It is a wonderful campus with plenty of disc golf-able area.

My brothers and I enjoy a good game of disc golf. We take turns picking a target, announce the 'par,' and go to it. On one hole, my brother Jon and I ended up in a small wooded area, off of the intended path of our discs. I was barefoot and wearing shorts, he was in pants and wearing shoes (as I recall the story).

Guess who got poison ivy?

Wrong! He did. Funny how quirky genetics can be. Well... when it comes to our family, 'quirky' can be used in so many sentences.

~ ~ ~

Hence, I was entirely unconcerned about poison ivy as I wandered through this small area of woods. What I was concerned about was finding my favorite disc. The woods weren't very wide, and there were fences, about six feet high, along the southern edge of the park. On the other side of those fences were residences. As I saw it, the disc might have gone in one of the two closest yards. Both had doors on the gates, but I wasn't real sure how they would feel about someone using those gates from the park side. Chances are it had happened dozens of times, but... how did I know? Out of desperation to find my favorite, I did open one of those gates, look both directions, and close it again.

Nothing.

I don't know how many times I walked through those woods, using my feet to shove foliage around, looking down for this little, precious, blue disc. From one end to the other, I walked through, looking all around me. I swept from one side to the other, one end to the other.

Once I was startled by a fat, juicy spider on my shoulder. Startled, I say. "Why was I startled?", I asked myself. I had gone through plenty of web. He probably had good reason to be visiting. Couldn't be helped.

Several times, I returned to the launch pad, turned to look at the field, and tried to imagine just where the little thing had floated away so easily. Then, I would begin walking as exactly along that path as I could remember it.

~ ~ ~

This last week I was in a room with several 'macro writers' — folks who, like myself, had spent considerable time creating macros that go into our company's varied systems, pull data, and bunch it together as requested by a customer (or by one's self). For me, it is all I do at this point. When I began doing it around a dozen years ago, I did it like many of the people in the room—as needed, to help with my 'normal' job.

But, for many years now, it has been my job. When I was first hired, some doubted that such work would fill forty hours per week for years and years. Well... they were right. It fills fifty with relative ease.

At any rate, early on we only had 'green screen' from which to pull data. Some readers may know that as 'screen scraping.' People would contact me from New York, Boston, Sacramento, Topeka, Denmark, Tokyo, or … wherever, and they would ask me, "Can that be done?"

The answer was *always* Yes. If you could see it on a screen, there was a way. I *never* failed to believe that. Back then. It wasn't really a belief in myself, but a belief that, *yes, Virginia, there is a Santa Claus*. I knew that if it was on a computer, there was a way to retrieve it and put in a document for further review.

That belief hasn't really changed in the last few years as we have lost more and more 'green screen' data points, but my belief in the ability to obtain the data myself has. I am not the brilliant individual that people think I am at the office, but a reasonable facsimile.

I have a friend who was also in that room of developers. I frequently acknowledge him when it comes to this kind of work. *He* is the brilliant one. There isn't anyone in the company who is better at what we do than he is. *Nobody.* Mine is the name people may know, but behind most of my work, somewhere, there is a bit of his pre-work. When it comes to the original accessing of a system, he is *The Man*. After he gets in, he shares his work, and I take off and do oodles of things.

So, I still believe *"It Can Be Done"*, but it isn't always by me.

~ ~ ~

But *this moment,* here in a small wood, required the It Can Be Done spirit of old.

Honestly, I prayed. You bet your bottom dollar I prayed. The prayers were not always very mature, but I prayed. Yes, there were actually some of the "why?!" variety. That's crazy, I know. But we live in the moment, do we not?

And, frankly, I am not much of a believer in the "God doesn't care" philosophy. I read this thing about sparrows once. And I wanted my favorite disc back.

~ ~ ~

My son Ian tells a story about persistence.

At Scout camp one summer he was given a project. Given the materials he had, he and a buddy were to make a patrol flag. Nothing special, just a flag that they could call their own.

The problem was—he wasn't given any materials. There he was, in the woods, no materials in hand, and he and his buddy were supposed to make a flag.

"I can't," he kept saying.

"Go do it," was the persistent response.

He was frustrated. Even angry. But... he got to thinking about it, rather than simply repeating, "I can't." And... that flag is now in a box in our attic. He seems to have made a breakthrough in his life during that little scenario.

It was a "It Can Be Done" moment which would last a lifetime, even change a life.

~ ~ ~

I kept looking. Sure, I could walk away, but *the thing still existed*. If it wasn't in one of those yards, it was still *here*. If it was in one of those yards, then someone must have come to get it, because I didn't see it. So I was sure it was still here. Unless Star Trek technology existed, it was still here. In the woods. Unless it was disintegrated, it was still here. It had to be here. And, if it was here, I was going to find it.

~ ~ ~

If I remember right, I originally bought it in Rockford, Illinois. My oldest brother had picked one up, was using it when we were out playing, I got my hands on it, *really* liked it, and wanted to find one just like it. Eventually, I did. And I have had it ever since. Maybe it has been more like twenty years.

When I felt like it was lost forever, I texted all three of my brothers. My oldest brother, Dennis, understood the dire need to find the thing. Losing a good golf disc was not a good thing. It was a veritable tragedy.

And, to make finding it even more imperative, my old phone number was on it! Even if someone found it, they would not be calling the right phone number to return it.

~ ~ ~

Prayers, again. After all, it was getting dark.

As I prayed, I reminded myself that the thing *had* to exist. Disappearing wasn't an option.

So, I began to look upwards more often (by 'upwards' here, I do not mean prayer, though that continued, too). About 35-40 minutes into my search, I found my disc—about 7 ½ feet up in a bush.

~ ~ ~

Persistence can be pretty easy, really. It just takes time.

Well… it also takes *belief*. In those early macro-ing days, I always had that behind me—I believed that it could be done. Without that belief, the persistence would not have been as easy and carefree as it was. Without the simple belief that my favorite golf disc still existed, I may never have found it, because I would have ceased trying.

Without the simple belief that God *did* care about silly things like a golf disc, I would never have had that long conversation with him about a golf disc… which led, actually, to this whole writing. Because, If God doesn't care about a golf disc, why would you?

This whole week of business travel had been somewhat trying for me. I was in a room full of people who seemed to think I was something extraordinary—something that I very much was not. Because they had benefited from my work for years, they believed I could easily swing into this new world of data and make their lives easier once again. The main problem was—I didn't believe it.

And, there in the woods, as I found myself believing in some pretty basic ideas, and, due to the persistence of belief, found my favorite golf disc, … I reluctantly began to think that, maybe, what was really missing in my work at that point in time was my own belief that It Can Be Done.

So, returning to my hotel room, I sat down at my laptop …
and dug in. Persistently.

Butterfly Providence

A wiffle ball bat. Two wiffle balls.

I pitch.

Sometimes I get it by them; sometimes they hit it past me.

This time there were two balls behind the batter—lost in the bushes.

He found one.

They aren't massive bushes. He'll find it.

I stand in place as a butterfly passes me in its fluttering flight. I watch as it flitters in the air between me and home plate.

A butterfly flies forever. There is no desire for speed. Every flight appears to be naught but pleasure.

The batter hasn't found the ball. Two fielders join him in the search. Something tells me, though, that they will not find it... quite yet.

The butterfly plays with more air, quietly approaching the plate. It does not hesitate to fly where pitches and line drives existed mere moments ago. It butters the sky with gentle wings.

I watch as this little play of Providence unfolds for one tiny, beloved creature.

Sure enough, as it reaches a place in the yard's sky where no ball will go, the batter cries out, "Here it is!"

And the Father, who knows when the slightest sparrow falls, has given a butterfly long life and a pitcher two minutes of wonder.

Bee Hives Down & Manhood

There is little fear in this child. Not even the healthy kind.

Well... having watched him calmly jogging through the garden, attempting to escape the attention of many very irritated bees, perhaps I'd have to say that he does have a healthy fear—at least of a bee's sting. Or, as in this case, the stings of thirty bees.

But, this moment of fear was an anomaly for him.

~ ~ ~

I still remember the day I looked out the back door of the house and saw what was then an 11 year old boy flying out the front door of the barn.

On a rope.

Upside down.

Such scenes had been common with this child. So, when he wanted to take up beekeeping with his mother, there was no reason to think it would not be a fun trip. Buckle your seatbelt, Dad, and enjoy the ride.

~ ~ ~

The wind storms that Friday evening came rather quickly, struck hard, and left behind a welcome change in temperature. For a few hours.

Before the storm, we had all been doing normal Friday evening things. Books, papers, pens and pencils had been reminded that they had homes. The living room floor became more visible than it had been since Monday morning. Floors were swept. Educational tapes and cds were shelved or drawered once again. The entire house was preparing for our oldest son to return home sometime during the weekend. A family movie later in the evening was a possibility, after the cleaning.

With all this activity going on in the house, I walked out to the garage to put away a few things. I looked at the yard and gardens, which remained desperate for water. We had been putting off watering for three days. Rain had been in the forecast, but the promise continually broken.

Walking the 50 feet from the house to the garage, I felt an eerie sense of impending doom. There was something odd in the air, in the feel of it. I looked into the chicken yard to find that the hens were generally moving toward and into the chicken house. Darkness was not approaching, but...

Something was coming.

~ ~ ~

A while back, a friend of mine was standing in his kitchen with his wife when something outside their window caught his attention.

A tornado.

He and his young family went into an inner room and listened as their house was demolished around them. He later remarked that,

A)	They experienced no "calm before the storm", and

B)	It did not sound like a train

~ ~ ~

Eerie. Yes, that was the word for it.

Five minutes later, all the calmness of the air was gone. The winds had come, and they were crazy. Within a minute of the beginning of the storm we saw a large part of a tree lying across the front yard—near one hive. That hive suffered no harm, though, even after part of another tree came down nearby.

Ah, but the rain, sweet rain, had finally come.

Horizontally.

I heard one of the kids say that two hives were down. They had been knocked over. By the wind.

What?! How could that possibly be? Each box weighed around forty pounds, each hive had three or four boxes. How could wind do this?

Those hives were the two we all would have thought the least likely to suffer such a fate. Their position was well protected from the West wind by both our garden shed and our large barn. We had hives on the NW corner of the barn, in the front yard (near those limbs I mentioned), beside the chicken house, and behind the corn crib. Any of those would be more likely to get blown down. None of them did. Only the two in the safest place.

Then, as the storm was in full force, This Child wanted to go outside and fix the hive situation immediately.

He was restrained. For a time.

~ ~ ~

Lately he has been bugging me for a motorcycle. A typical conversation goes like this.

"A motorcycle?"

"Yeah, Dad, it would save money."

Ha ha. He would try to lure me into this trap with arguments I would appreciate. I was always trying to get the car up to 40 mpg. I was a Sunday afternoon driver. On weekdays.

"Not a chance."

"Why not?"

He wanted reasons, but none of the reasons I gave him settled. Not that I was surprised by this—his ears were not as open as they once were. He knew Mom and Dad were the end of the matter for now, but didn't necessarily agree with their reasons. That's okay... all that dust would settle in time.

Me: reason, reason, reason.

Him: excuse, excuse, excuse.

Me: "The answer is no."

He may be exasperated right now, but... reason would prevail. He knew, too, that my "no" wasn't necessarily permanent. My reasons being what they were, a motorcycle wasn't out of the question *in the future*, but it was entirely unreasonable in the *now*.

~ ~ ~

We watched out the front windows as our recycle bin flew by. A couple containers that had formerly held bee suits on the back porch flew by—empty. Hmm… that meant there were bee suits somewhere, too. Two old plastic 50 gallon barrels the kids used for barrel-walking and standing on rolled from the backyard, through the gardens, and across the field. One rolled towards the road, until it was stopped in the ditch just prior. The other rolled into the fence, then parked.

Old shingles were flying. What? Our house didn't have old shingles. Ah… old shingles, which used to be under the metal roof of the barn—which was, for the third time in eight years, being shredded by winds. I guess we'd have to fix that. Again.

The storm's winds began to die down a bit, but there was still plenty of wind left when my wife, This Child, and I went out to do what we could for the hives. When we got out there, we could see a pile of bees lying in the grass, the various boxes from the two hives knocked down, some things upside down, and we could clearly hear and see the metal barn roof pieces flapping in the still strong winds. My mission, as the dad, was to get this job done and my loved ones out of harm's way as soon as possible.

The two beekeepers with whom I worked? They were oblivious to the flapping metal with exceedingly sharp edges—including the pieces which were already lying on the ground of the barnyard.

Prayers happened at all times.

Out there in the blowing wind, getting drenched, picking up boxes filled with angry and frustrated and confused bees ... I was having the time of my life, but prayers were definitely flying. Who else gets to live moments like this? How in the world could life be more enjoyable than moments... like... these? Exhilaration is the word.

Lord, keep those sharp metal pieces away from my family. I sure do like having them keep all their body parts.

~ ~ ~

The Mrs. had her full bee suit on, This Child and I had gloves. I cannot even remember whether This Child and I were barefoot or not, but barefoot would not have been a good idea—just the quickest idea.

We picked up boxes, set them upright, but only on the ground. For some reason one of the beekeepers decided that upright on the ground would do for now, rather than up on their stands. I went to pick up one box, heard the quick yell of caution, but... too late. I had picked up a box upside down, spilling out the angry contents. Picking them up as quick as was reasonable, I set each of the frames back into their home again, and set the box where it belonged.

As the boxes were back upright, my attention was again drawn to the flapping razors overhead. I urged the others to get done and get back in the house. Finally, whether it was because they saw reason or because they didn't want to put up with my urging any longer, they succumbed. We returned to the house. We had done more than what was reasonable, but less than what would need done when the weather settled. The hives would be fine, but the beekeeper's work was not done.

~ ~ ~

Back inside, drenched, but satisfied, we'd had our excitement for the evening. I had some stings on my feet, maybe elsewhere, my son had stings on his head and face, and would have some minor swelling in the next couple days. But those stings said something to me—about manhood, about willingness and readiness to do something for those outside himself, even to his own pain.

What more could a dad want? What more could a man ask of his son?

This, my friend, is manhood.

And here, in this oft-not-reasonable frame, was a young man.

I am thrilled and proud to have him as a son.

Bird in a Bath

I see a bird
standing in a puddle
in my driveway.

It dips into the water
stands upright again
and shakes.

This process is repeated
several times.

Then, satisfactorily cleansed,
it flies into the sky
to resume its day.

As do I.

I confess
again and again.
Cleansing
Like a bird

Then, I fly into my day,
clean,
refreshed,
and thankful.

~ ~ ~

Matthew 6 is a passage that comes back to me over and over and over again. I absolutely *love* the line in which Jesus says, "Consider the lilies of the field..." Jesus is speaking to some specific issues—our daily anxieties, our scratching and desperately clawing after wealth or basic needs, and He instructs us what to focus upon. But, hidden inside of this teaching is a *wonder* that has struck me for many years.

Jesus is teaching us something about life through the natural world that actively flies around us. In a way, he's not *only* calling us to identify our need to stop worrying, or to focus on the right thing, but to follow his lead in this kind of reflection. "Consider the lilies..." He calls us to reflection, to contemplation. He calls us to emulate something about the nature of Jesus which we tend to forget.

I imagine Jesus spent some of his carpenter downtime, or his Sabbath afternoons, dwelling upon the wonders that surrounded him. In those wonders he saw aspects of the Father, principles and precepts of life, things we were intended to *understand* by the nature of the world around us.

I imagine an enthralled Jesus sitting in a field, observing a colony of ants carrying food in and out of a hole. He may think of the Proverbs that tell of the ant, or he may simply watch the ants. He soaks in the amazing selflessness, the constancy, the harmony of this little world. He watches for an hour, maybe more, then suddenly he "comes to" himself, and he laughs, realizing how far the sun travelled while he stared at an anthill.

Perhaps he looks up and sees sparrows flying. Instantly spellbound, he lies on his back in a field to watch. His able mind, unfettered by the sin which tangles our own, understands what he sees, has understood these things since the first time he enjoyed the site. Unhindered by sin, his mind works more quickly, fluidly, and rightly than our own. He understands those birds in a scientific way, but that doesn't reduce the joy of the *poetry* of what he watches.

He understands them poetically. Flight is remarkable.

He admires the beauty of a simple bird. He sees every color in the feathers, the sleekness that allows the water to fall off, and the lightness of those amazing legs. Seeing the form, the feathers, the tiny eyes, all the marvels that have been lavished upon this tiny creature, he is reminded of the Great Sculpture. In the bird, Jesus sees aspects of his Father that frequently elude the most religious of people, blinded by their lawyer-like attentiveness to a law not written for the reasons they think.

His heart hurts for the blind, even while he continues to see in full and living color.

Yes, I imagine that. I imagine that out of sessions just like those, some of Jesus' most beautiful and resonating teachings have come across the centuries to us. And, I *seek* to wonder, to observe, to learn from the natural world. I see his infiniteness in the sky, feel his power or gentility in the wind, taste a hint of his depth in a glass of wine, and observe his independence in a cat, his loyalty in a dog.

~ ~ ~

The bird is on an electric line
Far out of my reach
Even on the edge

Of my aging sight

But he has filled more purpose
This contemplative morning
Than he knows

His cleanliness has reminded me
Of my own need for the same
His flight has reminded me
Of *life*

And... I consider...

Civic ≠ Bulldozer

She was laughing. In fact, it might have been describable as 'uncontrollably.' Not just laughing, but laughing *at* me. I could understand. Given my situation, it was perfectly understandable.

"Okay, wait," she said. "It can't possibly be what I think you just said. Can you say it again?"

I went through the brief story once more. Laughter. Maybe not quite as much as the first two times, but... Honestly, I love her laugh. I've always loved her laugh. But I sat confined in the car waiting for the laughter to subside.

Finally, she said she would get help sent my way, and I hung up the phone.

As I sat in the car waiting for assistance, I thought back through my day. I am sure everybody has their days. This particular day ... may have been... one of mine.

Perhaps it had really started the prior evening. One of my sons had a debate coaching session near Columbus, Ohio. It started at 5, ended around 9. We didn't arrive home until nearly 11.

That is *way* past my bedtime.

So, when I found myself quite awake around 3, and realized that my mind was already off to the races, I rolled out of bed and got ready for the office.

Slowly.

In our main bathroom, one of the kids (or is it my wife?) has a small basket hanging from a cabinet knob. I wouldn't put it there. Inevitably, it will get bumped, fall off, and it will have a 50-50 chance of falling right into the toilet. One little bounce and that thing could throw the toothbrush and all the other things into the dreaded and questionable sea.

Which is mere inches away.

Well... that morning, that foreseen "little bounce" happened. Then and there.

In the shower I have a routine. Wash hair, wash body, brush teeth, shave. Then, grab towel, dry off top to bottom, dry feet prior to stepping out. I never let my wet feet touch the floor. I always do it like that. I do not even think about it. There is no variance. I've gotten out of the shower having *not* done one of those things before, but those moments are rare and typically due to sleep deprivation. And, when they happen, I know something is messed up as I get out—I can feel the lack of continuity.

This day, I forgot to shave.

Having already dried myself off, I got back into the shower and finished what hadn't gone quite right. Dry off again, with my wet towel, step out of shower, get dressed...

How could I have forgotten a shirt last night? Well, rather than wake my wife up by re-entering our bedroom and opening my closet door, which is right beside her side of the bed, I'd find something, *anything*, hanging in the laundry room.

In the mornings, if I am in a situation in which I do not want to make noise, I also don't want to create wonderful breakfast smells and have those smells wafting up the steps (I know I can wake up to good smells, not sure about the rest of my dozing family). In those moments, I grab this little shaker-bottle and create a reasonably healthy eggnog—2 eggs, a little sugar, dab of vanilla, fill with milk, shake. Sometimes the kids don't get the pieces of my shaker bottle put away quite right, so it may take me a moment to find the right pieces.

I try to do this carefully, because I do not want to make too much noise—especially on this day, at 3:30 am. I found the bottom piece right away, but I could not find the top, or the piece that goes inside to help in the shaking / mixing process. As I inched my way around the shelves … I only broke one glass on the floor.

I froze. There were words in my head which did not belong there, but I refused to let them out.

After freezing for a moment to listen for waking persons, I turned on a light and carefully cleaned up after myself. Sweeping the broken glass, quietly sliding it off of the dust pan and into the trash, I knocked over a can of I-knew-not-what.

Bonk!

A moment of silence, in hope.

Then, milk, 2 eggs, sugar, vanilla. Dern that vanilla. It wasn't supposed to pour out that aggressively.

With everything in my hands, I quietly left the house.

If I say that again, will it work?

With everything in my hands, I *quietly* left the house.

Dangit. No change.

With everything in my hands, I attempted to leave the house quietly, but failed when I dropped my laptop on the floor.

Whew. At least it wasn't the eggnog.

Then the door gave the shelf behind it a good 'bang'.

Lord, help me.

With everything in my hands (again), I quietly left the house. This time I mean it.

One of my sons once had the ambition to be a Ranger. If he did so, and if he carried any of my gangly and clumsy genes, he would die on his very first mission.

As I was saying, with everything in my hands, I quietly left the house. On the way to the car, I was shaking my bottle of eggnog when the lid popped off.

I stared at the eggnog flavored snow in the moonlight in silence.

After a moment of mostly-silence, I picked up the lid, put it back on, got into the car, and put my empty breakfast bottle on the passenger side floor.

Forget breakfast.

Who needs breakfast.

Freaking breakfast.

I started the car, and began heading out the driveway, only to discover that more drifts had occurred the night before. Hmm... could I make it *through* the drifts if I picked up a little steam?

Sure!

I did. The snow was fairly light, so I barreled through it with no problems.

Let's see… that probably makes the score: Life 8, Me 1.

Or something.

Out of the driveway, on my way to work.

Did you know that rabbits are on the road at 3:39 am? I didn't either. That one would stay on the road for a while yet.

Things didn't really go badly at the office. I'd been working on fine-tuning some of the programs I offer. That was actually going pretty well.

On my way home later, I realized I'd forgotten to call home and tell the boys that they needed to clear the driveway. It had been windy all day long, so I figured there would be more drifting. The other day I had used the van to 'crash' more space out at the end of the driveway. With all the shoveling we had been doing, we had been making huge piles of snow on both sides of the driveway's end. I took a picture one day when I needed to get out of the driveway in the Civic. When I had looked to the left, I could see nothing but that pile of snow.

Click.

When I arrived home it didn't appear to be too bad. Yes, there had been a little bit of drifting, but not too much. I assumed the snow would be light enough, like it had been the night before, and earlier that morning, that I could push my way through.

Assumed. Yes. You know what that does.

Yes, I had decided to use my Civic to do a little bit of plowing.

Hmm.

And... there I sat.

On the phone. Listening to my wife laughing. At me.

Having ignored common sense, ignored the fact that my Civic was *not* a bulldozer, nor a pickup truck... I made my feeble effort and found myself totally surrounded by snow. Yeah, I moved some snow... just enough to let me get right in the middle of *all* of it.

Bummer. Having crawled around several parts of the car in order to try all four of the doors, I gave up. That was when I made the phone call, asking my wife to send the boys out to shovel me out of the driveway.

The car was stuck. I had learned how to drive in Minnesota back when I was a teen in high school, so I knew how to rock a car out of such situations. Having tried to do so, I had thoroughly locked myself in-between all those walls of snow.

The doors were held shut by snow drifts. All of the doors.

Maybe, in time, Angie and the boys will forget this story.

Front Porch Ramblings

If I were to chase a dream
Knowing that dream would succeed
The dream that I would chase
Would not be individual success

I'd not write that book I'd hoped for
Nor build the house of my wife's dreams
I'd skip creating that retreat place
I'd hoped to provide to the world

All the hopes and dreams of my youth
The wonderful and lofty thoughts
Subjugated to a Higher Will
Reduced, in fact, to ashes

With certainty that a singular passion
Would pay dividends in the end
I'd pour my heart and soul
Into the lives of my children

To see them walk into Eternity
With joy and love divine
There's nothing this world has to offer
Than this simple and fantastic fate

All else would seem trite
In comparison to this one thing
I can know that I am called to
Unlike any other endeavor

Such success is not guaranteed
But why spend my life
On any other endeavor
Than to disciple, train, and nurture

Those who have clearly
Been set in my life for
And over whom I have
Undoubted influence

My Awkward Encounter at Starbucks

Over a year ago I met with a friend from work for lunch in Columbus. I had helped her on a few items, and she wanted to treat me to lunch so that we could 'catch up,' as well as to offer a bit of a 'thank you' for the things I had done to assist her. While we were there, she gave me another thank you—something I had never thought about having.

Two five dollar Starbucks cards.

I wrote a Facebook status later that afternoon saying: "I have a minor dilemma—someone just gave me 10 Starbucks bucks, but I don't even know where one is..."

I probably had more of a variety of people comment on that status than I have on any status since—most of them volunteering to remove my dilemma by gladly receiving said cards. What are friends for, right?

Not knowing what to do with the Starbucks cards, I gave one to my daughter—who had a Starbucks at the university she was attending. Then, I put the other in my car and figured I'd use it eventually. I had been told by one of the many friends who had written that there was a Starbucks in my local grocery store.

About 5 months later, my friend from work contacted me about something else, but included the question, "Did you ever use that Starbucks card?"

I asked, "Do they expire?"

Probably not.

Still, on my way home I thought I'd make use of it. Knowing that things cost a ridiculous amount of money there, I figured I'd have a little bit of change left on the card at the end. So, I prayed, "Father, put someone behind me in line who could use the leftover part of the card." I'm sure nobody who is going to Starbucks *needs* the dollar or two that would be left, but... perhaps such a small trifle could be an encouragement to someone.

When I walked into Kroger I had one other errand, so I passed the Starbucks spot (which was entirely empty, except the two employees), and went to handle my other errand (banking... so... why is it that I can walk into a grocery, do two errands, and not even do *any* grocery shopping?). After the errand, I returned to Starbucks and found it *still* empty, except the two employees.

Hmm... I wondered, how am I going to get rid of the extra?

I approached the counter, only to discover that there was not an obvious place to approach. The entire counter was filled with extra gunk. Goodness. How do I know where to walk up?

One of the employees asked me if they could help me. I was staring at the board, with about 16 items available. Remembering the *one* time I had tasted from Starbucks— when my daughter had purchased a stiff something-or-other when I was leaving her at university one night late— that is, well beyond my bed time. I couldn't help noticing that *nothing* on the board seemed anything like it.

"Uh... I had something once that was a mint chocolate something or other..."

There was a pregnant pause (what in the world does that mean, anyway?) as she waited for me to do something other than stare at the board with my mouth gaping open like a cod fish.

"Well," she finally broke in, "the closest thing we have is a peppermint" something or other. I don't remember what she said. Several words.

I continued staring at the board.

"Uh... okay."

"What size?"

"How much is a 16 oz.?"

The other employee punched some keys on the cash register and said, "4.35".

Ohmigoodness.

"Okay. That."

I handed him my five dollar card, which was suddenly almost entirely spent.

Then, I stood there. At the counter.

He handed the card back, with a little piece of paper that said how much was left—65 cents for those of you who should never work behind a retail counter. He then asked whether I wanted my receipt.

I thought I had my receipt.

"Uh... uh... no."

The lady behind the counter asked me if I wanted whipped cream.

"Sure."

The guy back there said something.

I didn't catch it. "What?"

"Your drink. It's ready."

I looked at him blankly. If my drink was ready, how come he didn't hand it to me?

He pointed to the other end of the exceedingly cluttered counter. There was an oval table-top on the other end. On it sat my exorbitantly priced "coffee" thing.

"Oh!"

I turned to see whether anyone else had gotten into line. Yes! A young man was waiting for me, the un-Starbucks-clod, to move so he could order.

I asked, "Do you come here often?"

"Yes," he said with a smile.

"Here. I don't. It's only 65 cents, but I know I won't use it."

He actually got excited. *Excited* over 65 cents of a Starbucks card. He thanked me. Exceedingly.

I stepped over to get my Starbucks coffee thingy, the lady told me to have a good evening, and I told her the same. I saw those little heat-protector things, grabbed one, correctly unfolded it, and correctly (I assume) installed it around the base of my cup.

That guy thanked me again as I walked out.

I began to drink it. Hmm. Frankly, I could make something that tastes better at Speedway for 99 cents.

I drank about half, and saved the rest for Angel, because I thought she might like it better.

When I got home, I handed it to her. She sipped.

"Ew."

I guess not.

The boys drank the rest.

I'm not really a coffee drinker anyway. If someone asks me how I like my coffee, I typically tell them I like my coffee to taste like a doughnut. And, with prices like they have for coffee that tastes like doughnuts, I'm probably better off without the habit. Besides—I can make coffee that tastes like donuts for free at the office. A packet of hot cocoa, a cup of coffee, voila!

At Christmas, a group of work friends from out West sent me an eighty dollar gift card for Starbucks.

Oh boy. Here we go again.

Oh, also, I'm now much more familiar with Starbucks.

Like many people, I often 'suffer' from depression. I generally find my own depression coming from one of three categories:

1. A lack of real faith—things about the Gospel which I claim to believe, but which elude my mind in my darker hours. I tend to forget simple things like mercy, my 'identify in Christ,' and the like. Forgetting these things, I wander into my own foolish darkness, then, by the mercy of God, remember.

2. Sometimes it is based in my own inaction, my frequent lack of fruitful activity. When I face depression, I am most often reminded of a conversation which happened between God and Cain, back in Genesis 4. What I see there is a man who is not living right, and, hence, his countenance is down. The Lord offers a simple approach to correcting this problem—if you do well, will not your countenance be lifted up?

   • And the Lord had regard for Able and his offering, but not for Cain and his offering. So Cain was very angry, and his face fell. The Lord said to Cain, "Why are you angry, and why has your face fallen? If you do well, will not your countenance be lifted up? And if you do not do well, sin is crouching at the door. Its desire is for you, but you must rule over it."

3. Ingratitude. Sometimes I find that the simple practice of gratitude is very helpful in shoving depression off the surface of my life.

4. Other times, I do not shake it off until I begin to take action on a necessary project or endeavor—as though I am filled with depression simply out of my own unwillingness to face tasks which I do not wish to face.

Though I understand that not all depression is based here, I know that much of my own is. This time my own depression was sitting in #1.

My Gospel-Telling Window

As I finished putting the last finishing nails in the last trim boards around the window, I stood back to look at the 'finished' product. Yes, there were mistakes. No doubt. I could tell from the opposite doorway that I'd botched the cut or measurement or calculation on the windowsill itself—there was a quarter to half inch difference between the left and the right sides. That would drive me bonkers, but... others probably would not notice. In fact, I'd already heard from my wife—she didn't see it.

I did, of course. And I felt like I always would.

In a conversation earlier that day I had mentioned that I knew why I would never build a house. "I will always know that I am surrounded by my own mistakes."

My daughter wisely said, "Dad, that isn't even theologically sound."

Heh. True.

These last several days I have, once again, found myself on the downward spiral of depression. Sometimes I see it coming, sometimes I don't. I saw it coming this time, but... couldn't get my finger on what was going on. The last time it came on me I texted my wife when it was coming. It was ethereal to be able to pinpoint it like that, but it was sort of useful.

I sat upstairs at my desk a few days back, in the midst of my latest funk. Turning around, I saw a book on my shelf that I had forgotten all about—*Spiritual Depression*, by Dr. Martin Lloyd Jones. It had been recommended to me by a pastor friend a while back—when I had stopped in to visit him in another time of depression. These times had been coming too frequently these last couple years. After our little meeting I'd come home and discovered we already had that book on our shelves, though I did not remember how or why. It may have been something one of us had picked up at a used book sale.

The other day, I began to read it. In fact, I know it was only two days ago (even while my older two were home for Thanksgiving weekend), because I arbitrarily decided to read a chapter a day, and I'm on the third chapter as I write.

I'm finding that I already know much of what I'm reading. It isn't like the information is *new*, but... that doesn't imply that I do not need to hear it. Again. What I'm reading takes me back to that house full of mistakes.

I remember a home church moment from several years back. We were meeting at a local park, in a shelter. A dear friend sat with his family off to my right. He mentioned something about how unworthy he felt. With all the love and adoration that I had for the man, I simply looked over at him with a smile and said, "You're right—you *are* unworthy."

He smiled in his large way, and was encouraged. We both knew what I was saying. And it helped us both.

I am a father of six. I own an old farm house, several beat up old out-buildings, and a few high mileage vehicles. We have old chickens, a dog that has lasted over a decade, and cats in plenty. A kitten sits on my lap as I type. The dog sits to my right, sleeping in her old age, not even budging as the smell of pizza wafts into the living room. A Christmas tree is lit off to my left, my wife sits in front of me reading a book on her Kindle, and everyone in the room is getting pizza. My daughter sings quietly to herself while doing homework for college—where she will return early tomorrow morning. Kittens fight near the fire, which a nine year old has diligently kept alive all afternoon.

My house is filled with mistakes, but the house is also filled with love, mercy, and grace.

That is where my theology strayed. That is where my theology tends to stray the most. I will *never* earn the peace and joy that I am given, because my life will always consist of innumerable mistakes.

There will always be too many kittens.

There will always be scratched paint on the floor.

There will always be measurements not quite right.

There will always be...

There will always be...

There will always be...

But Grace prevails.

There will always be ... Grace.

That last board I put up by the window had come with a story. For the two trim boards beside the window, I had to 'rip' two boards. That is—I had to cut them from end to end. The boards were nearly 5.5 inches wide, but I needed 4.5 inches. That was what I needed in order to match the many other old trim boards in the downstairs part of the house. "Ripping" didn't seem like much fun. It made me sweat, in fact, though it was chilly outside as I did the work. It was a bit dangerous—something that required some *safety* efforts. Shoving 5+ feet of board through a table saw, with the intention of reducing it from 5.5 inches to 4.5 inches in width, may not be as major as I make it sound, but, then again, I hadn't done anything like it since high school under the good supervision of a shop teacher.

Well, when I had cut the windowsill itself, I'd made some mistake which I didn't realize until I'd nailed the thing in. That being my 5th attempt, I decided to keep it. I'd checked with my wife first, to ensure that it wasn't that visible. She didn't think it was, so I accepted my error as permanent. I knew I would notice it, and forever, but... accepted it.

When I ripped the two side pieces, one of them got slightly away from me near the end, so it ended up slightly more narrow on one end.

Well, I thought, Grace prevails.

See, I took that narrower part of the board and set it on the down side of the right board. That reduced the apparent-ness of my earlier mistake. I could not help remembering, then, that God often uses even our mistakes as He works out the fruit of our lives (see Romans 8:28).

And, now and ever after, that window will not only be a reminder to me of my own mistakes, but of the Gospel itself.

My error, my sin.

His Mercy, His Grace.

Win, win.

SDG.

Love—Infinite and Unbounded

Were they not my own lips that mocked Him?
Weren't my hands those which struck?
Was I not one who blindfolded him
Then demanded he tell us who hit?
Was I not numbered among the blasphemers?

Was I not counted among his false accusers?
Was I not one of the maddened crowd
One who asked for the release of Barabbas?
Did not these lips cry out, "Crucify Him!"?
Wasn't I one who laughed at Herod's mocking?

These hands that crushed down that thorny crown
These hands that hammered in each nail
These lips which scorned and mocked
These feet that kicked

This heart was blacker than the night.

And yet, absurdly, I bore no guilt.

~ ~ ~

I lie awake thinking of the dreadful scene. But in all my
imaginations I never step forward to lend a hand, never try to
stop the horrible injustice that occurred before my restless
mind. It was almost like I could not step into the scene on His

side, but only against Him. As though I, like the disciples, had been pronounced beforehand as one who would deny.

The blood spatters on me
as the whip comes across His back.
I'm frozen in the moment
blood tasted on my lips.
The blood.
It stirs my soul.

I wake. Tears are in my eyes. Vomit stirs in my throat.

I want to soak in the entire scene. My heart longs to more fully comprehend His suffering. I want to understand it more, and more, and more again. I suspect a perfect understanding is not available here—on this side of Eternity. Even were I to experience unfathomable physical pains, I would not be able to understand perfectly what he experienced.

No, some thirsts will not be filled. Not here. Not now.

Among the infinite numbers of things He accomplished in the Crucifixion was a simple but profound and impossible to fully comprehend lesson—a lesson of Love in the face of Hatred.

I wish I could spend a billion words telling of that one lesson, but I will eventually need sleep, and that ultimate example of Love is spattered all over the scenes of my dreams.

Instead, I will lie in bed and consider:

- The Heart that Loved in the face of Hatred
- The Husband who Loved the Bride who scorned Him
- The heart of this writer, which was designed 'in the image'

There is no Death that is free to hold me back. The love I have to give need not know any bound, for I draw it from an Infinite Source.

Mark's Ordinary New York Adventure, sans New York

Sometime last fall the boss said that I should go to New York. She generally gets what she wants. So, I had to go to New York.

First, though, I tried to talk her out of it.

Attempt #1

"Boss, I've already done everything I can for this project. Without that software that records my steps online, I cannot take this project any further."

"So order the software."

Drat!

Two days later, after finding out that I am not allowed to order software to use on internal systems without getting approval from Congress, which, at the moment, was rather busy creating more debt for Americans born after 2115, I contacted her again.

"Boss, I can't order the software without going through an extensive red tape nightmare that is unlike anything that has existed since the days of the Pharaohs of Egypt. They want my firstborn, 6 quarts of blood, half of that in ink, and thirty-four future draft picks of my beloved Cleveland Indians. Oh, and for a lot of documentation to be completed. I don't do documentation. I'm a programmer, not a legislative branch."

Still un-perturbed, the boss pointed me in the direction of the group admin, and said, "Go".

Dernit. Now I have to start filling out paperwork in order to buy a 150 dollar software package that only *might* help me get deeper into this project from *heck*... pardon the language, but it had to be said.

Attempt #2

"Boss, it will cost the company more than 1600 dollars to take me to New York. Why would we pay that kind of money when I've already done pretty much everything that I can do on this project?"

That didn't seem to faze anyone. Not only was my trip going to cost more than 1600 dollars (prior to taxi fares, food, and the expenses incurred with three dozen interpreters who were there to help me decipher taxi-cab-speak), but the boss was going, and her boss was going. Why? Because I was going. Apparently having me go was a big deal. There were people in New York, working for our company, who were fainting just knowing that I was coming. I'm apparently rather famous in those parts—rock star, they say.

Obviously, they all need to get refunds on their lobotomies.

Attempt #3

"Boss, we are getting two new loads of chickens at the house."

I could see the puzzled look on the other end of the phone line. After a pause long enough for me to prepare for flight, she said, "What did you say?"

"Chickens! We are getting more chickens at the house, so I should probably be there to help get things in order."

Again, I could see the puzzled look on the other end of the line. I could also hear the "click" and that annoying nobody-is-on-the-other-end-of-the-line noise.

Attempt #4

Lots going on in my life at the moment. A group discussion I'm leading on Saturday morning—eight hours after I am *scheduled* to arrive home; another class I'm teaching on Sunday morning—for which I'm probably more prepared than I let on; and the first of 15 weeks of classes on Thursday—for which I'm somewhere between totally unprepared and more prepared than the average boll weevil.

Never mind. I won't bore you with the details, but I did leave a message on your answering machine to let you know that I'll be on flight 2181 from LaGuardia to DC, departing at 1603 hours, arriving at 1716 hours, having traveled 214 miles, plus the 34 times I'm sure we'll circle DC as we wait for the president's most faithful minions to quit protesting against air flight while former veep Gore is circling the globe in a private jet telling people to stop using so much energy. Oh, and to leave a message telling you that I was calling you from the bushes outside your house. No worries.

~ ~ ~

In the end, she took no excuses. So, I prepared for a trip to New York. Unfortunately, I was vacationing in the DC area while all of this 'preparing' was happening. In the Metro. Between stops.

Oh, and less than 24 hours after returning home to my beloved Ohio I'd be sitting in an airport in North Carolina wondering why I was sitting there 'on my way' to New York.

~ ~ ~

So, off to New York.

Have you been to an airport lately? It is, quite possibly, the closest most Americans will ever come to experiencing the Crusades in our time. I don't mean the "evangelizing the heathen" part, either, though I'm thinking that's probably the very thing many of those happy TSA agents need most.

No, I mean the torture part. You know—the part where a graying (shut up), 46 year old white male walking with an obviously hobbled knee is looked at as a terrorist, but the 24 year old man of obvious Middle Eastern descent who looks angry, carries an M80, six machetes, and more large bottles of shampoo than your local Walmart, is passed through security like a prince. Yeah, that Crusade. That part, I mean.

So, as I walked through the line of shoeless people, took off my belt (wait, what?! Are people now hiding explosive devices in thin leather belts?!), watched a 94 year old woman in a wheelchair get taken to the strip search room (I admit, she did look a bit dangerous), counted my spare change, gave the prison warden the evil eye, …. You probably don't need to know the next part. Suffice it to say, I thought colonoscopies were nasty, but… no, really, never mind.

Later that week I was waiting in the 'lobby' of the Dayton International Airport, watching and listening. My flight was to be from DAY to Charlotte, then on to NY. Admittedly, that seemed a bit out of my way, but it was better than the Dayton to Dallas to Anchorage to Subic Bay to Kazakhstan to Siberia to Cleveland to Sydney to Paris to Venezuela to NY route. I mean, really, who wants to have a stop-over in France? Have the airlines always taken these bizarre turns? How does this happen? Is it the pilots?

"Bob, I know we're going from Dayton to New York, but I need to stop over in Pakistan for a moment to see my brother about a land deal."

"No problem, Ahrmanadubadamed, no problem."

So, as I sat there, I tried to get some reading done, but everything around me was so interesting. There appeared to be only 13 of us heading to NY. Well, I guess that's assuming they were all going through Pakistan like me, but... whatever. There were 13 of us who were boarding the flight for wherever the pilot wanted to go before dropping us off in NY. Oh, yeah, I mean Charlotte.

As I sat there, true story, the news on one of the 25 monitors at DAY (that part might be an exaggeration), told of two passengers who had been hospitalized *in Charlotte* (insert heightened alertness here) after a turbulent landing (insert mild fainting spells here) just moments before (insert whatever you'd like, I don't care, because I can't concentrate at this point anyway).

At the same time I'm hearing this fun trivia, the dungeon workers who weren't slayed by TSA on their way into the office announced that my airline had cancelled a flight to Washington DC due to weather.

Then, a few minutes later, my airline announced they had cancelled a flight to Philadelphia due to weather.

A few minutes later, my airline announced they had cancelled a flight to Boston due to weather.

I waited…..

And … they didn't announce it. Apparently, MY flight, which was now known to be heading for the Land-of-the-Doomed, NC, wasn't cancelled.

I chuckled out loud. Heck, what else could I do???

There was a time when the thought of turbulence, just the *thought*, would make me feel green, clammy, and slightly chaffed. There was a time when air travel itself, the thought of air travel, made me curl up in the fetal position (why do we call that curling 'up,' by the way?), close my eyes, and chant, "There's no place like home. There's no place like home. There's no place like home." There was a time when releasing my luggage to three men dressed like mafia dons (who appeared to be packing more than my unused CCW permit would allow) would make me vomit in my own shoe. (after all, I was still carrying it.) There was a time when….

What was I saying?

……….

Er… oh, yeah, it was time.

"Sir?" A woman with bleach-blonde hair, leather skin, and Tammy Faye makeup was trying to break through my thin veil of sanity. "Are you alright?"

"Of course! Why do you ask?" I'm not sure why my voice cracked.

"Well, you are curled up in the fetal position, appear cold and clammy, and you have been chanting."

"Oh. That." [Nervous chuckle] "Of course! No, I'm fine."

As she walked away, I'm pretty sure I heard her mutter, "Why is it that we say 'curled UP'?"

The time had come. The time for all sheep to be led to the slaughter was nie. Ny? Nigh? Yeah, nigh.

"May I have your attention, please. We are now boarding flight…." Their politeness was clearly a ruse.

I looked at my cell phone. We were only an hour late. That's okay, I thought, they expect me here two hours early, torture me about the weather, search my under garments for things I now wish I possessed, and now we are hours late. That's okay. I'm happy. I won't cause any problems. I won't say anything offensive to the nice Russian security guard on my way onto the airplane.

No, I will go quietly.

After I received just a few more fresh sneers, I was sitting on my first airplane in almost a decade.

Flying. Ah, yes, the great time saver of the 20th century. I had left the house shortly after 3:30 PM, driven the 30 minutes to the airport, trudged through the airline counters, dropped off my baggage and firstborn, gone through the Russian mob's intrusive search procedures, taken off articles of clothing I had not known existed, received oddly shaped paper bags from total strangers who asked me to deliver them to relatives with complicated names and no addresses, danced the chicken dance with a shoeshine boy, drank 86 ounces of caffeinated fluids, watched re-runs of the news of passengers near death in Charlotte, written four copies of my last will and testament, had visits from three priests for last rites, been interviewed by the FBI, testified at the mafia trial, gone through the witness protection program, run for congress, and now, finally, here I was, sitting on an airplane.

What a pleasurable experience it had all been.

Why hadn't I done this sooner?

Moments later, we were cleared for takeoff. I felt my whole body tense up (why is it we tense 'up'?), felt cold and clammy and green, vomited in my shoe, and spent the next hour and 17 minutes chanting.

Then, we landed. Without turbulence. In Charlotte.

I was halfway to New York.

The following piece is, admittedly, a bit dark. But it is real in its own way. I think that we all have lonely times—even those of us with friends and family surrounding us, as well as a vivacious faith.

As you read, perhaps you will find yourself here. We all hide a bit, at least sometimes, but when we open up to those around us, when we allow new degrees of vulnerability, we can experience something other than increased pain. We can taste joy.

SDG.

Veneer

There is a thick sheet of veneer
That we all wear like varnish of the soul
We do not want others to see below it,
Except for brief glimpses
A brief glimpse gives the viewer just enough of a view
Of our brokenness to let it seem noble

I see myself sitting at a table—a long, wide table
Far away, at the other end, you sit
You cannot clearly see the wrinkle of my brow
Nor the scar on my chin
Nor the gray in my hair
I hold you that far away
Because it protects me from the intimacy
That closeness demands

I sit at this table with you
Because of the intimacy it pretends to be

Sometimes my soul is like those hideous plastic bags at
the grocery
I long for Quiet, to be able to sit in Silence
But those bags keep rustling
That noise isn't severe, but
It is not Quiet
It is distracting
It is disruptive
It breaks the Peace that my soul desperately longs for
It is... harsh... maybe even Evil

You walk past, but I do not see your eyes... not really
I am looking straight at you
You are looking straight at me
But... neither one of us is revealing anything
I don't know why you aren't
But I am not really thinking about You
As much as I am thinking about Me

I want Something
There's Something that I want
I am not even cognizant enough to ask
Whether You have It
Nor do I ask
Whether You know what it is

At our table I look towards you
My eyes burning with the hunger
That I honestly feel

Is there anything there?
Do you have anything to offer?
Are you any different than I?
Do you feel the same thing I feel?
Are you hungry, too?
Are you looking for Something?
Do you know what It is?

I am trapped. Somewhere.
Where am I?
It is dark
It is ... shallow
It is lonely
It is ... it is not good
I am scratching at a wall
Calmly, at first
But with increasing alarm
With panic growing
By the day
I cannot get out
Claustrophobia is nothing compared to this
Where am I?
Why is my pulse quickening?
It is getting hard to breath
I am getting desperate
I am getting frantic
I am ... breaking down

Where am I what am I doing here how did I get here what
questions do I need to ask what answers might there be is
anybody out there can somebody help me I do not know what

help I really need help me oh please help me someone
somewhere somehow

My veneer remains
Somehow it even hides Me from Me
How can that be?
Does anybody really see me?

I am crying
I do not really know why
It is just too complex for me to comprehend
So many variables
Roll into the complexity
That is Me
Is it the same for You?
Yes, I suppose it is
But I am not really thinking about You...
At least... I wasn't

Those bags
They are still rustling
Please make them stop
Please!
I ... I cannot focus
Please make them stop
I need them to stop

The wall
Won't go away
How am I going to get out of here?
Why can I not get out?
Can someone please get me out?

I do not want to be here
Please help me out!

Hello?

This table
So big
So long
You
So very far away
I stand up...
But I am not sure why
You are still way down
At the other end
Of the table

The rustling!

I realize that I am standing
You are still way down ... there... I...

Those bags!
Make them quit!
Make them quiet!

You walk by
I catch your eye...
And I hold it
You hold my gaze, too
You stop walking

I am still standing

At the other end
Of the table
You are standing, too
I see the wrinkle
In your brow

Someone stop the bags
This is important

There's a crack in the wall
Some light is coming through

I look at your face
You have been crying, too
For the very first time
I sincerely wonder why
I honestly think of You

I begin walking
Down to your end
Of the table

I reach to touch
The tears
On your face...

I break a hole in the wall...

I reach my hand out for yours...

I do not hear the bags...

And I wake.

The pregnant cat that wasn't

I kind of like order.

My family, on the other hand, isn't a fan. It isn't that nothing is ever in order, but… I'm pretty sure that they aren't as interested in it as I am. On some days it feels like it simply has no working definition in any of their minds. I say things about it from time to time.

Things like:

- Drawers are meant to be closed when they are not in use
- Cabinets are meant to be closed when they are not in use
- Dirty socks are not welcome on the living room floor
- Dirty socks are not welcome on the couch
- Dirty socks are not welcome on my lap
- Dirty socks are not welcome on the computer
- Dirty socks are not welcome on the television
- Dirty socks are not welcome on my shoulder
- If you don't pick up that dirty sock and dispose of it immediately I will throw you out the window
- [grunt] Somebody open the window
- This couch is not a book shelf
- This couch is not a table
- Why is there an open pocket knife lying on the chair?
- This couch is not a storage area
- I would like to sit on this couch
- Did I mention this couch wasn't a table?

- I want to be able to walk through the hallway at night without risking death or impalement
- Did you know your bike doesn't go right in front of the door?
- Did you know I found it there on my way out the door at 6 AM?
- Why are there three coats, six cups, three forks, and two plates in the van?
- Would someone please remove the chickens from the laundry room?
- Table. Clean it. Especially the dead bird of unknown origin
- Who was in my closet?!
- Hallways are not for storage. That's why you have a room, a closet, cabinets, and access to an attic.
- Whose stuff is this on my nightstand?
- Why are there two tents set up in my living room?
- Why are there two tents set up in my living room?! What am I saying?!

Perhaps you get the picture, but I really could go on and on. Trust me.

I really don't think that "I have a problem". I simply like, and have the unreasonable (it seems) expectation of, order. How about ... once in a while?

Well... keep that picture. One Friday I walked into my house and found those two tents set up in my living room. They were not in their handy little storage bags, which, of course, were lying randomly on the floor. They were standing up. In my living room. Between the two couches—which, of course, had to be moved for the seven millionth time in order to make room for the two tents.

"Why are there two tents in the living room?"

All I got was a casual and dismissive hand wave.

I've been at this a very long time. I am a veteran of such occasions. I know exactly how to handle these situations.

I walked upstairs with a sigh.

~ ~ ~

We have a history with tents. Last summer, for example, there were two tents in the front yard. Forever. I would say, "Is someone going to *sleep* in one of those tents?"

There would be general... ignoring of my question.

I would wait.

Days.

I would go move the tents, so that the grass beneath them would not be obliterated.

General consternation would ensue.

I would wait.

Days.

Weeks.

I put the tents in the barn without taking them down.

Nobody noticed for three days.

~ ~ ~

My simple idea is this—if you put up a tent, you better sleep in it.

Seems simple enough, doesn't it?

Anyway, there were two tents. In the living room (not sure I'd mentioned that). I asked Will and Silas whether they were going to be sleeping in either. Silas said he was.

Alright... I figured I would join him.

For varying reasons, that time did not come until last night.

Last night I got into this tiny little tent, folded myself up into somewhat of a contortionist position, and quickly realized that the 'padding' that my dear nine year old son had laid out was just enough to fool me into thinking that there was padding laid out. Other than that, I was lying on a hard wood floor. This would be swell, I thought.

The moment I laid down, just inside of the tent door (I figured I should be by the door, because I'd be getting up early in the morning for work), our dog laid down inches away from my head, on the outside. I managed to keep her entire body outside of the tent, but that didn't mean much, because smells know no doorways.

Silas was almost asleep.

In front of him, in front of his curled up form, laid our pregnant cat.

Until around 11:30 pm... when she ceased being pregnant.

Whut.

~ ~ ~

Silas had warned me.

"I think she's going to have her kittens tonight. She's acting kind of funny."

Indeed she was. She was being friendly and almost cuddly, purring. A funny Agnes was not a good thing, because it surely was a sign. She was typically not a friendly cat. She was not very relational, with us or her kittens. She was not a lap cat. She tended to mind her own business and only come talking to us when she wanted food or water. Else, she talked to kittens if they were hers. She kept talking to kittens, in fact, for a many days after they were all gone to new homes.

Tonight, as I laid there allowing my bones to create molds of my hip, knee, chest , and shoulder in the wood floor for posterity, I heard rapid purring that indicated to me that something was amiss.

I was pretty sure that Silas didn't purr.

The cat didn't generally purr, either, but especially not when nobody was petting her. Hence, I knew it had to be coming. Why not, I wondered, because I hadn't slept anyway.

Then the tiny voices started. And I do not mean the ones in my head (those were later).

Kittens. One voice. More purring. Another voice, licking sounds, more purring...

I wasn't going to look or care how many there were. She had a history of large cat herds. Eight once. What kind of cat gives birth to eight little ones in a night?

The poor thing was giving birth. I'd let her have her privacy— right there in what would be Silas's lap if he were awake.

11:30 PM.

11:49 PM.

12:03 AM.

.

.

.

.

12:37 AM.

I was not asleep. It wasn't the tiny voices (not the ones in my head). It was the wood floor.

Silas was asleep. How do kids do that? There is a miraculous birth experience occurring *in your lap, buddy*. And you are sleeping. I am clearly jealous. And I don't want any kittens in my lap.

I got out of the tent, tried to work around the dog, and moved to a nearby couch, blanket in hand. Before I was lying down, the dog was on the end of the couch, lying where my feet ought to have been.

1:02 AM.

1:13 AM.

1:17 AM.

.

.

.

.

.

2:00 AM.

I hadn't heard the furnace all night. It did seem a bit chilly. And... something told me...

I got off the couch, on which the dog was now quite asleep. I had hoped to let her keep sleeping, because she often follows me everywhere I go in the middle of the night—unless I am following *her*, because she also likes to wake me at 2 and 3 and 4 and... any time, so I can let her out for a moment.

Anyway, I tried to offer her that courtesy, though she never offers me any courtesy.

The thermostat in the hallway said that we had left the heat on 68. Unfortunately, it also said that the temperature was now 64. I headed for the basement.

Earlier in the evening... well, technically, the prior evening, now that it was "morning," I had been in the basement cleaning out something in our furnace. It needed to be done every couple years and I had reason to think it needed it again on that particular day. While I was down there I had heard a *snap*—like an electrical *snap*. Perhaps a *zap*? Anyway, it didn't sound like a good thing, but I didn't see any reason for it anywhere at the time. I did smell a wee bit of a smoky smell, but... didn't see any signs of harm or damage. The house wasn't going to burn down. But... who knows about the heat.

I figured that may have come back to bite me. Which it had.

At 2 AM—when the temperature was down to 64 degrees, there were kittens in a tent in my living room, a young boy sleeping on a hard wood floor, a dog whimpering at the top of the basement steps ("Shh!"), and all other occupying humans slept in their own beds.

"Oh, Lord, don't let it be that little thingamajig thing."

And how would I know whether it was? I thought the sound (and, maybe, *flash*) had come from the other end of the furnace the prior evening, so I focused on looking there. I didn't see anything out of the ordinary, but when parts go bad do they really give off warning lights like a game show? I think not. That would make replacing them entirely too convenient, inexpensive, and do-it-yourself-able.

Still... I had the thought—what if it was simply a fuse?

I checked the fuses. Sure enough, we had one labeled "furnace". I flipped the switch off on the furnace. I unscrewed the fuse. It looked burnt. I had a 30 sitting nearby. I replaced it. I flipped the switch for the furnace.

Poof. It worked again. Oh, sorry, I didn't mean 'poof' as in 'zap' and stuff. Didn't mean to frighten you.

"Thank you."

Back upstairs. Let the whimpering dog out. Wait a bit. Let non-whimpering dog back in. Walk towards the couch only to have the crazed, skittering of dog feet going back and forth as she attempted to guess where I would lay my head... it is a little game she plays. She wants to be where I am, but she's frantic about getting there. I am not. So, she typically makes a mad dash to where she's guessing, which is inevitably *not* where I am going. Then, she dashes back towards me when she realizes she guessed wrong the first time. And, frequently, the second time. Etc.

Sometimes I purposely go where she doesn't, but only so I can get onto the couch and under a blanket as quick as possible before she jumps on the end of the couch and prevents me from getting humanly comfortable.

Which she does.

I do love my dog, but...

I finally fell asleep on the couch with the tiny sound of kittens coming from the tent in the next room, a nine year old boy sleeping in his tent, a dog lying at my feet, and a mind wandering through yet another book idea, a prayer, some quiet gratitude for such a ridiculous life, and verses it grasps for when it hopes to find sleep soon...zzz...

When I woke, I realized that the tent would be in the living room for as long as six weeks.

Zoikey.

Life Appreciation (aka, Epilogue)

When I was in my second college experience, back at UALR (University of Arkansas at Little Rock), one class I took was "Art Appreciation." The professor was a middle aged man, tall, lanky, glasses, a bit effeminate, and a generally nice guy. He was the kind of professor who wanted to be liked by the students, he wanted to be popular. I do not say that as an insult, though it may suggest some personal issues, but as a difference between he and some professors—those who really didn't care two cents about the average student's existence.

He was also one of three professors in that first year who were *clearly* from the liberal side of the political aisle. In spite of the fact that I was clearly a conservative, I had very good relationships and conversations with all three.

One of the others was a writing professor who tried to persuade me to major in writing. I chose not to do so, because I couldn't see such a major leading to the paying of bills. My wife and I had chosen years earlier to have a big family, to have me in the workforce earning our income, and for her to home educate our children. So, being a writer, in my opinion, wasn't going to cut it.

One of the other professors was a card-carrying ACLU member who taught my Political Science course. We had some great discussions—especially in the middle of class periods. Those discussions were possible due to the fact that we had mutual respect for each other, in spite of our political differences.

Of course, *neither* of those professors are the topic of today's little chat....

~ ~ ~

Art Appreciation class. As I recall, the class was one part Western Civ, one part Philosophy, and two parts Art History. There were times in class when I had the "light bulb" moments—when I saw why certain kinds of art were happening at certain times of history, alongside philosophical schools of thought, alongside quirky actions on behalf of the State. It was all woven together ... just like it is in our awful philosophies, art, and government today.

One day in class our professor put a picture of some plain, ordinary, everyday things on the wall. As I recall, the gist of the remarks, by students as well as the professor, had to do with how "mundane" and "drab" and "ordinary" everyday life was, and how the artists were trying to portray it as such. They were choosing odd things to paint—pictures of pots, of wall paintings, kitchen tools, etc.

At the time, I was the young father of only two children. That was precisely *two* more kids than I needed to recognize that "everyday life" was anything *but* mundane, ordinary, and drab. So, up went my hand.

"Mark."

"If that is what the artists were trying to convey, I think they failed. Even in this picture, there are details that are fully capable of striking at our emotions and stirring us." I pointed out some of the things in the picture which had the ability to intrigue the student of art.

"I just think that everyday life is something wonderful, beautiful, and extraordinary."

I heard some quiet agreement from behind me—an older student who didn't have the same zest for stirring things up as I did... apparently.

We talked in class, then, about parts of the picture—the way the artist had used shadow, the items that were selected, the room in which the items were painted. I told some "little" stories from "every day" to indicate just how *not menial* everyday life was. There was laughter, there were other stories told by others, and ... well, in the end, I think there was agreement—on my point.

After class that day, I had several people come and talk to me—more than I would on a normal, ordinary, drab, mundane, menial day. Everyone had a little story. Everyone *got it*. A cord had been struck. Music was playing.

~ ~ ~

I wish I could say that day was "normal" for me, but I cannot. I *rarely* inspire folks to think of their lives in larger, more precious, more beautiful terms. I'm typically the guy who is carrying the dark cloud, looking between the lines of the worldview, analyzing, scrutinizing, and generally pickling the thoughts of others.

Honestly, that's where I live. Even though I like to think that the primary message I've attempted to communicate in this life (and in this book) is *the wonder and beauty of everyday life*, as well as the *high calling of our everyday work,* I often find myself walking under a dark cloud of my own making. My *desire* is to help people to see that God's intention for this life is much broader than the myopic and unscriptural "we breathe in order to evangelize" vision of the modern church. I have made some of that clear, I hope, in some of what I have written. It's my hope that even in the stories I tell here I am suggesting to you, dear reader, that there's *abundant life in Jesus*.

I realize that my craft is nothing in comparison to the old masters. What I write will not sit on shelves in the year 2077, the pages will not become dog-eared, and libraries will not order new copies long after I am gone. There may be a copy on a shelf somewhere long from now if that shelf belongs to someone in my bloodline—someone who, like me, looks back through the fog of time at an unknown ancestor, happy to know that *somebody* in the family wrote and published.

But, honestly, this little book isn't a Dickens, a C.S. Lewis, a Dostoyevsky. It is simply me, Mark Cheatwood, making my little effort to say something to your soul, hoping to convey a piece of the *wonder* that is available all around you, and hoping, honestly, that you will come to know Jesus.

As one old musical master put it:

SDG

27156289R00103

Made in the USA
Charleston, SC
04 March 2014